Advent 2013

God's Gift of Love

Scriptures for the Church Seasons

Advent 2013

God's Gift of Love

DONNA SCHAPER

An Advent Study Based on the Revised Common Lectionary

Abingdon Press / Nashville

GOD'S GIFT OF LOVE
by Donna Schaper

An Advent Study Based on the Revised Common Lectionary

Copyright © 2013 by Abingdon Press

ISBN-13: 9781426767999

Manufactured in the United States of America

13 14 15 16 17 18 19 20 21 22—10 9 8 7 6 5 4 3 2 1

Contents

Introduction 7

Move Beyond the Time Famine 9
(Isaiah 2:1-5; Romans 13:11-14; Matthew 24:36-44)

Preconception, Reconception, and Conception 17
(Isaiah 11:1-10; Romans 15:4-13; Matthew 3:1-12)

Sacrament: Finding the Holy in the Ordinary 27
(Isaiah 35:1-10; James 5:7-10; Matthew 11:2-11)

Scavenging for Advent 35
(Isaiah 7:10-16; Romans 1:1-7; Matthew 1:18-25)

Love Is Born 43
(Isaiah 9:2-7; Titus 2:11-14; Luke 2:1-20)

Leader Guide 51

Introduction

Advent again! This guide is about how to hark it, mark it, bark it, and lark it even when we may want to snark it. The last verb is not just for rhyme. It is this writer letting the reader know that she dwells just an inch outside of sentimentality. Sentiment, yes. Sentimentality, no. The sentiments evoked here will all be gifts of *love*, a word that turns to sentimentality almost as quickly as a sandwich with mayonnaise goes bad in the sun. I am snarky about sentimentality and awed by sentiment. You don't have to become fully ironic if you are slightly ironic.

Sentiment is the sensational experience of loving and knowing you are loved. Love as a sentiment is as moving as a red hawk in flight, one that comes close enough to let us see its striated feathers. Too close and it would scare us. Too far away and we can't even see it. Love as a sentiment as the real thing, the really real, has to be careful of mushiness. Love has to come close enough but not too close. When too close, we fear the loss of our self. Too distant and we can't experience it. Because God is love, God chose to come as a baby, in a careful, quiet approach, on tiptoes, so as not to scare us.

Babies don't scare us, except when we worry that we are in charge of their vulnerability. Advent doesn't scare us either because there is always the chance that we really have 40 days, four weeks, and yet another candle. Eventually, we will see the gift and love of God in our midst. We don't have to worry if we forget to open some of the little doors on the Advent calendar or open the doors to our lives.

There are so many ways to hark this Advent coming of the love of God that we may find it hard to choose. Choosing allows us to enter the love of God through the time famine, that awful sense that we will never be good enough, never have enough time, or miss the love as it flies over. Why were we on our cell phones right then? That first week of letting time and God love us will be followed by a second week when we begin to conceive what it means to be free of the time famine and full of a new kind of time. The theme will be conception; the command will be to conceive. The third week will be a nudge toward the sacramental, the permission to find the holy in the ordinary. The fourth week will find us scavenging the love. You do have to look for the unlikely in the unlikely place.

If the first week is about becoming free to receive the gift of love, the next three weeks are steps after realization. We are loved! We may conceive, sacramentalize, and scavenge for surprise. Nothing is wasted on us. Then we come into the Christmas time and texts themselves; and there we hark, bark, and lark and forget snark. There we live in a peace that passes understanding because love has found us. In that time, we know the peace, love, and joy for which we have sacramentally prepared. We are ready to conceive God's love in us. We are pregnant with possibility. We know love, not as sentimentality or even sentiment. We know we are loved.

Move Beyond the Time Famine

Scriptures for Advent:
The First Sunday
Isaiah 2:1-5
Romans 13:11-14
Matthew 24:36-44

In my family, we celebrate Christmas, Hanukkah, the Jewish New Year, Passover, and Easter. My husband is Jewish, and I am Christian. We've been this way together for thirty years. Some people rest on the minor holidays, but I usually have to work because parish pastors work opposite of the regular workweek. "Can you see me on Columbus Day? It's the only day off I have until President's Day." Couple requests like this with "Mom, why can't you go to the beach with us? You are always working."

If clergy were the only people living in time famine, especially around the holidays, maybe I wouldn't complain. But I don't know anyone who doesn't say, "I don't have enough time." This is a universal lament, which is as much about death and dying as it is about living. The poor join the rich, Jews join Christians, men join women, and adolescents join octogenarians in this great sign of our time and times. We are the richest people in the world in many ways, and yet we live in a time famine.

Indeed, we don't have enough time. Our days are numbered. Advent is the cessation of the numbing numbering and the beginning of a different kind of counting. Advent shows us the way of peace, of sword changing into iron plow, of pointing to the unexpected in each hour, of understanding Jesus, who told us that the time for the Son of Man to come is unknown. Best we wake up, as Advent admonishes. Best we wake from our sleep, which keeps us in the dark, and get lit. This chapter is about how to get lit. It is for the person who doesn't want to say, "I am burnt out." It is for the people who know we aren't machines and aren't burnt out. Instead, more truthfully, we are not even lit. How could we be burnt out?

Advent people put on the armor of light against the time famine of darkness. We have a spirit of joy that edges out the spirit of anxiety. We are the people who choose, digest, and chew. We are people who get nourishment from a way of being in time. Instead of acid reflux from too much fast food, we maintain a diet of peace, quiet, calm, and joy. Advent can show us a way to move out of a time famine into a time feast. In this chapter, we see how to get from having a time famine to a time feast by turning the sword we now use on ourselves into a plow that aerates our spiritual soil, by waking up, and by learning to expect the unexpected.

ABOUT THOSE PLOWS
ISAIAH 2:1-5

Isaiah 2:1-5 offers a hopeful and peaceful vision to Judah and Jerusalem during a time of political turmoil and attacks from other nations. The vision is sharpened with the images of the swords and the plows in verse 4:

God will judge between the nations,
  and settle disputes
    of mighty nations.
Then they will beat
  their swords into iron plows
  and their spears into pruning tools.
Nation will not take up sword
  against nation;
  they will no longer learn
    how to make war.

A sword is a weapon that finishes things off or threatens to finish things off. Many of us don't have real swords, but we do have weapons we use against each other and ourselves. We close down, close off, or live with the great anxiety that today will be the same as yesterday. We say unchristian things like, "It will always be this way," "Nothing can change," or "That's just the way it is." We do violence equal to that of the sword to ourselves. We become infected with anxiety. We abuse the days we do have. We inoculate them with a persistent pessimism. Because we have no hope of peace or sense of satisfaction, we live through the time famine of never being good enough or having enough as though it was a permanent condition. We actually consent to the bad news about human beings and create more bad news.

An iron plow is a different kind of tool. It plows. It aerates. When we pick up an iron plow, we act out our hope that we will be fed, not famished. This tool grows things. The promise of the Old Testament lesson for Advent is that we can and will grow. We will be fed. We will stop the great sword of war as well as the small sword of self-flagellation. We will get out of the great stagnation into a beautiful economy. We will plant seed in soil, and that seed will flourish because of the hope we plowed in with it. With every second we give to the sword, we are hurting ourselves; but with every second we give to the plow, we are helping ourselves.

Advent is not simply a 40-day holiday or season. It is more like a process. The sword finishes things off quickly; but the plow slowly, steadily creates and opens space for new possibilities. I love Advent and don't particularly like holidays. Holidays have sword-like tendencies. They imagine all the joy, peace, and hope will be on a certain day. They offend the gardener in me. They have a tendency to become a time famine themselves, especially when we try to do too much.

To switch the metaphor from an agricultural one to a culinary one, Advent is a process of marinating and preparing. The holidays yell peace and joy at us, but Advent prepares us for peace and joy. During the preparation, we become the ones marveling at a God about to be born. In the shouting, we are frequently disappointed by all that the holidays promise but don't deliver. The time famine is the takeaway of the holidays much too often for many people. Advent promises a time feast.

Planning can help. People say they don't have time to plan because they are so overwhelmed by the things they were supposed to do yesterday and didn't do. Planning to put the sword down and pick up an iron plow—or planning to marinate in the moments you do have—can help. It just takes a second to hope. I often describe that second of hope as a turning. People talk to me about how defeated they feel, how they don't dare believe that anything good could still be possible for them. I often ask them to simply turn around. Just turn around. Look back at something good that happened. How did it happen? Why do we waste our time beating ourselves with swords? Could we expect just a small thing, just a look up or around or back or over?

The word for this kind of turning is *reflection*. Lives that are all action and no reflection yield a time famine. Lives that balance action with reflection yield a time feast. Can we give a second per minute to reflect? a minute per hour? an hour a day? Why not? I know the e-mails are waiting. I know the house is a mess. I even know that you think if you were just more efficient then you'd have a better job, a better resume, or a better report for the boss. I also know that you will get each of these by reflecting on your next action and strategizing your next move, rather than just doing, doing, doing. The biggest proof of the value of reflection is the mess many of us feel our lives are already in. Why continue doing what we have been doing? The same inputs will yield the same outputs. A slightly different input may yield a slightly different output. People who know how to use plows understand. We remember what happened in that part of the yard or garden last year. We pause to remember. We turn our behavior. We make a "not-to-do" list.

You do have time to plan. You do have time to move out of the time famine into the time feast. You even have time for an Advent process even while managing the stress of the holidays. You can do both, especially if you add an Advent process to a holiday moment.

Advent practice consists of plowing and marinating. Things taste better when prepared in advance and especially when marinated before cooked. I think of eggplant resting overnight in Tahini sauce, fish soaking in soy sauce, or meat rubbed in spices. I think of applesauce made from those apples I found on an August day. Maybe it is time to open the jar and have some.

Likewise, pregnancy is a process that prepares us for the awe of birth. Part of the process includes childbirth education class and training in breathing exercises. For me, it is no accident that God came as a child, through a pregnancy, which is one of the most awesome processes of all. God was strategic in sending the Messiah as a baby. In spiritual marination, we come slowly to the birth. There we marvel about how God could dare come as a child, send heaven to earth and spirit to flesh, or drench humanity with divinity. We taste the results before, during, after, and always.

When has the season of Advent seemed like wielding a sword? like using a plow? How can you move from the sense of famine into the feast of the season? What daily practice might help your "spiritual marination" for the birth of Christ?

A SPIRITUAL ALARM CLOCK
ROMANS 13:11-14

The time to wake up from sleep is now. This second Scripture of the first week acts as an alarm clock. It is not the unpleasant kind that wakes you up for another day of time famine, when you feel inadequate, overwhelmed, lost, or meaningless. It is instead an alarm clock that wakes you up for a day of adequacy, preparedness, and meaning. If you want to argue that the only day you like an alarm clock is when you are on vacation, about to take a hike, or get to hit the snooze button, I want to focus on you. I want to ask the question, What you are doing with your one fantastic life? Why give it away to obligation? Why give yourself meaning, capacity, and joy for only part of the time? *Ouch.* I know my questions hurt. Not all days can be rich with hope and expectation but more should be than not. Now we are really talking about Advent and its process of reflection. I am not using a sword on you. I am asking a question that goes to the alarm clock of this passage. It says now is the time to wake up from sleep. So let's imagine that this first week of Advent you will consent to a process, a planning process, and a strategic plan not for your company or your congregation but for you. Do you really have time to waste in sleepwalking your way through a dark life?

The year was 1973. The place was Tucson. I was the (slightly paid) youth minister. The youth group initiated a composting project to raise money to go to San Francisco for an urban-immersion trip. They raised their money by using the Arizona sun to decompose lettuce leaves plus an eggshell or two that elderly ladies demurely brought to church on Sundays. I'll never forget seeing those white-haired ladies, wearing hats, carrying garbage to church on Sundays. They were barely touching what they couldn't quite imagine touching. We mixed in every kind of other waste we could find and earned six thousand dollars the first year. We sold the bags of compost for one dollar each. The trustees were originally appalled by what was happening in the parking lot, convinced it would stink; but it did not. As they watched that youth group wake up, they changed their tune. They even funded the youth minister for another year. The dozen kids who went to San Francisco were changed by their visits to soup kitchens, shelters, the morgue, and more. They woke up, as do many people when they turn or when they move out of their safety zone.

In San Francisco at that time, the police were just beginning to hire female officers. The sergeant leading our tour of the police station told us that the new hiring won't work because women can't carry the 100-pound bag of sand in a straight line for thirty feet. "They are just not strong enough," he argued. That's when a member of the youth group, Carol, age 17, picked up the bag and carried it back and forth twice. Turns out, she worked with horses. She hadn't talked much during the trip, but she woke up to that challenge.

Some wake up because they see what is wasted become fertile. Others wake up when they discover that all people have some kind of strength. Most wake up by a slow, steady faith formation through participating in youth groups, questioning what they learned, and then going on to walk a strong, secure line for life without trembling, tumbling, or being afraid of their load. Many wake up because they engaged a process of dissatisfaction. They weren't happy with the way things were. They were discontent. They faced their discontent. They woke up.

I heard a story from an Australian pastor once that really affected me. The district in which he worked was getting poorer and poorer. People were growing more distressed, some even despairing in their distress. People started abandoning their cars in the church parking lot. They couldn't fix them, and they couldn't junk them. After the sixth car turned up, the church started a car repair business. Guess what happened? The parking lot cleared, junk became joy. The parking lot woke up, the church woke up, and workers woke the dead cars up.

Not everyone can work a job that they jump out of bed every day to do. Nor can everyone be in a family that is fully happy. But more of us can turn more discards and despair into dollars and days if we try. Waking up to human possibility is something everybody can do a little bit.

What is an important awakening experience in your life? How was God present in that experience? How does it inspire or challenge you today?

NOBODY KNOWS THE DAY OR THE HOUR
MATTHEW 24:36-44

Matthew 24:36-44 talks about the coming of Christ, referred to as "Son of Man" in the New Revised Standard Version and "Human One" in the Common English Bible. In this passage, we see a comparison to the people swept away by the flood in the story of Noah (verse 39). They were oblivious to their imminent deaths. It seems like an odd image for Advent and for thoughts about the One who comes and who will come again. We must be alert and ready. We must live faithfully in the tension between life and death.

Throughout the Gospels, we see this ongoing brush with death in the stories about Jesus' birth, ministry, crucifixion, and resurrection. Jesus the baby becomes Jesus the man becomes Jesus the Savior. Jesus the living becomes Jesus the dead becomes Jesus the living. Even doing something as lovely as singing "Silent Night" on Christmas Eve will not last forever. The candles will be extinguished, the cover put back on the organ, the hymnbooks rearranged in the pews. The show that opened will also close. The way Jesus lived, always opening every gate, refusing every lockdown, became the pattern for a life that cannot die. Your best moments will evaporate and so will you. My best moments will evaporate and so will I. The approaching of the end is known because we know it is coming. The hour is unknown because we don't know when it is coming.

Do you have time to ponder death? Do you get shocked if you get a call about the death of the baby soon after the baby is born? It only shocks those who haven't had children. Those who wake in the night with an infant next to them in the bed and fear they might have crushed the child and those who know how vulnerable you can feel carrying a two-day-old newborn around understand and are not shocked. I have heard that fairy tales are good for children because they recognize children are already scared. Adults are also already frightened especially when they are young parents in charge of those who are so vulnerable.

The quick brush of death with birth only shocks those who missed the part about the Christ child being different. His death glorified God. The shepherds didn't get it. The disciples didn't get it. I don't know why we should make believe we do. We can try, but we don't have to succeed. Does a theology of the now/not yet and the always–coming help us? How about the mystery surrounding birth and death? It helps me. What echoes from Matthew is that the ending doesn't so much happen as threaten to happen. We must be ready.

How can all this big news about life and death become an Advent practice or process for us? I suggest some options. Spend today thinking about your own introversion or introverts you know. Note that the holidays demand an extrovert. Tend the inner, the quiet, and the inside. Make it safe to come out and play. Some of us are rare butterflies during the holidays. We are caught rather than engaged in conversation. Release someone from the obligation of engagement and be quiet together. Death is quiet in the way that life is loud. Practice quiet as a way of practicing the unknown that you know is coming.

Also, consider the possibility that Christmas is about what we have lost as well as what we have gained or will gain. The art of going home for the holidays involves remembering those gone as well as those present. Spend some time remembering your losses.

Perhaps you might spend more than you have budgeted on one gift to someone you especially love and who will be amazed to find out that you are less stingy than they thought you were. Or perhaps you could surprise someone with flowers as a pre-Christmas gift. Why? You don't want to have any regrets about your personal extravagance when you die.

Think about the side dishes. Think about the strays that will arrive at your table. Become someone who attends the sides and strays, like a good sheep dog keeps the whole flock together. Why? Because you don't want to miss any chances to be generous.

Hum Christmas carols. Memorize their verses. Sing them in such a way that people in the grocery store will hear you. Why? You need to make sure you experience peace, joy, and calm before you die. Actually, you need to experience these things much, much more before you die.

My friend told me he was called to his friend's house during the last months of his friend's sight. The doctor had said his sight would be gone in a few months and that there was nothing more he could do. Thus, my friend made a last-minute visit to his friend. He wanted to see him before he lost vision. Actually, both friends wanted to see the other during the time they had left.

Do you have time to see the hawk flying over your head? Do you listen to tolling bells? If not, why not? Can you lay a flower on someone's grave, even if it is someone you never knew? Can you do something you've been meaning to do? Can you send an e-mail to someone you really miss?

Dr. Ernest Campbell, one of the ministers at Riverside Church in New York City, often advised his congregation to energize the usual rather than schedule the unusual. Deepen the moment. Cry over mashed potatoes on Tuesday night. If you have a dog, thank it for making such a big difference in your life. Look at your friend who is not losing vision with the affection for one who is.

The hour is unknown, which is why you want just the brush of death in each moment. Be ready. Otherwise, you will take for granted what can't be taken for granted.

When have you thought about the brush of life with death? What was it like? What feelings did it evoke for you? How can this awareness inspire you this week to live more deeply in gratitude for the gift of life?

Preconception, Reconception, and Conception

Scriptures for Advent:
The Second Sunday
Isaiah 11:1-10
Romans 15:4-13
Matthew 3:1-12

Advent comes into its second week. Our theme this week will be conception, that moment of fertilization when something begins. Last week was a guide to ending the time famine in our personal and social lives. This week is when you risk a new beginning. You hark a new beginning by calling it out to yourself and to others. You mark it by changing an ounce of behavior. You bark it by making loud what is often much too quiet. You lark it by being glad you have a second chance (or a 998th chance).

You could also snarkily think about preconceptions, or how our preconceptions often interfere with fertility. We get so bent out of shape by our previous injuries, miseducations, slips, or falls. In order to conceive the new, we need a reconception. *Conception* as an Advent term is a way of loving the light and trusting the light that is just over the horizon. It is also an antidote to injury, miseducation, and falls, even the ones that break bones and hearts. It is a mark to ourselves that we won't live in famine anymore.

The Scriptures will help us reimagine conception, or new life. Often our preconceptions—that is, what we expect—are cursed by what has already happened to us. These preconceptions get in the way of new life. Reconception or reimagining is different than preconception. It moves toward the conception of something new. The Bible readings for today illustrate these various approaches or impediments to new life.

Isaiah 11:1-10 promises new life from what seems to be a dead stump. Many people imagine they don't get another chance, but the Isaiah text says that even old trees get another chance. It tells of how a shoot comes out of a stump, by help of the Spirit.

In Romans 15:4-13, Paul offers a vision of inclusivity and talks about the relationship between the strong and the weak. He echoes Isaiah to show that the root from the stump of Jesse becomes the Messiah, Jesus. Again, there is not a preconception but a reconception, which lights the path of our Advent way. Something new is happening. It is loving and good. It will surprise you. It may even be that the weak lead the way or a shoot comes out of a stump.

In Matthew 3:1-12, John the Baptist urges all to reconceive faithful living and to let go of preconceptions about being children of Abraham in order to move toward a changed society based upon God's rule. "Who warned you to escape?" he asks the religious leaders who come to be baptized (verse 7). Here he is baptizing people at the Jordan River, and he declares that some of the people need to reconceive their ideas about being cleansed. Repentance and cleansing should yield fruit.

What did we preconceive this morning? Same old, same old? What did we expect this afternoon? Same old, same old? Is there something we are fleeing as well as finding in our daily life? At church on the second Sunday of Advent, what will we expect to see? Humdrum hymns, humdrum hope, humdrum happiness? Or do we expect a magnificent sermon, along with singing so strong that it brings a shoot out of our spirit's stump?

PUT A BRICK ON IT
ISAIAH 11:1-10

Isaiah 11 begins by offering God's hope for the monarchy in Jerusalem with the image of a shoot growing from Jesse's stump and a branch growing from his root. Isaiah's vision of a righteous king (verses 1-5) and the vision of God's holy mountain (verses 6-10) are greatly beloved by Christians who see the visions fulfilled in Jesus. They also offer views of what a reconceived life can be when nurtured by God.

An older gardener once told me I could grow new hydrangeas out of old ones by putting a brick on a stem. In the fall, plants are straggly and leafy, with shoots coming out of them all over. I put one of the longer stems down on the ground and slammed two bricks on it. In the spring, I discovered two new plants growing on their own. The stems had become new plants. Did I have to pound those long stems into the ground to assure new growth? Yes. Gentleness would not have given them the smash they needed to reach their roots towards new soil. They couldn't conceive without me getting in touch with my tough gardener side.

When it comes to new conception, of being willing to try a new way, often some kind of toughness is required. We have to smash up the old stem on behalf of a new one. This makes me think of people who don't get along with their children. Often the reasons are good. Someone on one side or the other has some preconceived notion about how things should be. The need for power can overrule love, especially in intimate settings. In the work setting, it becomes problematic for people who no longer feel they have control at their job. When relationships not only break but also appear to break the same way every year, it is usually time for a smash or at least a brick. Something has to stop before something new can begin.

Conception is the promise of a new way. Our preconceptions can often turn our hope into a concrete mixer. We just circle the same sand over and over; and if we do it long enough, we turn into concrete. We become ready to be in the same position for a long, long time.

As Advent comes into its second week, we may want to review our relationships. Have they become cold as concrete? Has the injury that has happened become the injury that will happen because we preconceive it so? What would be a reconception or a new conception? Tough people, the kind who long for tenderness to return to them, will take out the bricks. We will hope for something new in the same action and motion as we smash something old. No more, we say. No more, we say—not with hate but with hope. We need a new plant here. It will come from the root of the old because it has to come from that root.

Some people say they are divorced as if divorce was a true break from a relationship. We are never divorced from what the relationship was or who our partner was, but we can stop the old relationship in its tracks. We can grow a shoot out of a stump. The stump doesn't go away so much as reconceive itself. We may no longer be married to the same person, but we are rarely divorced from the shared past.

Our hope will yield the toughness to reconceive. We may have to stay away from the relationship that hurt for a while. But we always know we will go back (or forward) with a larger love in our hearts for ourselves and for our God, who loves us. We will not be hopeless as we break off what has become a stump for us. We will see the shoot coming out of the stump and find ourselves back in the world of love. From that world, all things are possible. From a world without love and without hope, nothing is possible, except a repeat of the same injuries. We hark the hope by looking for shoots coming out of stumps. We bark the hope by singing loud Christmas carols. We lark the hope by feeling the same sense of release and relief that the shoot feels as it navigates the bark of the stump.

We may still experience a moment of snark, of self-protecting, preconceived disillusionment. We have heard all this before. We have even tried before. We are out of "try"; or as my daughter said once, "Mom, I am *si se puede*-d out." *Si se puede* is Spanish for "Yes, we can." Many people have the preconception of "Yes, we can't." They are *si se puede*-d out.

What the shoot from the stump says for people who have tried too hard for too long is this: Risk a little light, a little growth, and a small conception. Change an ounce of behavior to start. Don't change a pound, just an ounce. See how that makes you feel. After all, it was a shoot that came out of the stump, not a whole new tree. I wager that you will feel like you've been on a lark if you change just an ounce of behavior. Start with having hope in one of your relatives. Have a little hope in your partner. Look at your past with fondness and use it to see hope for your future.

Those who have lived through the path of a massive hurricane understand that a lot of trees go down and no roots grow from their stumps. However, Isaiah barks a reconception to Jerusalem and to us: Even dead trees can rejuvenate. Listen to him say loudly what is so often kept quiet.

As we come out of the great stagnation, we have hoped for more valleys to become mountains than did (see Isaiah 40:4). We see failures, and then hope that failures are not prolonged. We hear Jesus' words over and over about dying to live; yet we are afraid of the slightest death, even that of a hydrangea stem. We imagine that we are accepted and loved if we do things perfectly and never hurt anyone else. People really are afraid of hurting each other, if for no other reason than the possibility of retaliation.

We are often ashamed that we have put up with such despair for so long. Shame is the full-body experience that makes us believe we might not be worthy of connection. Advent comes along to reconceive the love of God in us: We are worthy of connection with God and with one another. We are worthy of another chance. We are loved. We need not be ashamed of our trouble. We can find one old, worn-out "plant," such as a personal influence or relationship, and put a brick down on it. We can stop what it has been on behalf of what it might be. We can reconceive ourselves.

What can you put a brick on so that something new might grow? This week, what new behavior might become the new shoot, the new growth, and the new vision of who you might be as a follower of Christ?

WHEN STUMPED
ROMANS 15:4-13

The love of Advent is unique. It conceives a new way. Through the birth of Jesus Christ, the love is small becoming large. The love is universal and believes that people can get along even when they are different from one another. It is about Jesus' preference for the weak over the strong. It conceives a different setup for our social and personal arrangements. When it comes to God's love, ordinary nature and ordinary politics are inconsequential. They are not the way of God. Instead, the way of God is to bring life where there is death, to let the weak lead the strong, and to love what ordinary nature and ordinary politics do not. The shoot growing out of the stump defies ordinary nature.

In Romans 15:4-13, Paul presents his understanding of God's way of relating to one another. He specifically speaks about Jews and Gentiles. For Paul, the very idea of Jews and Gentiles living together in some new conception defies politics for a way of life called the nation of God. It is a mistake to read Romans 15 as anti-Semitic because it claims the possibility that all people can live together. It proclaims the power of God's love—love so powerful that it will reconstitute nature, politics, and the way we live together. Jews and Gentiles can live together. This way of life glorifies God.

Paul presents a series of Scriptures from the Old Testament to show that Gentiles are included in God's salvation: Psalm 18:49; 2 Samuel 22:50; Deuteronomy 32:43; and Isaiah 11:10. He repeats the promise of the stump of Jesse and declares that such small victories will yield strong leadership over all the people: "Isaiah says, 'There will be a root of Jesse, who will also rise to rule the Gentiles. The Gentiles will place their hope in him' " (Romans 15:12). Paul echoes Isaiah to present Jesus Christ as the ideal ruler who illuminates and fulfills the vision of Isaiah. Romans 15 meditates on strength and weakness, on harmony and encouragement, and on how encouragement yields power to lead. This text is political in the sense that God, through the servant-ruler Jesus Christ, empowers the people to cohere into one great nation. It is personal in the sense that God's action in Jesus Christ encourages hope in us. It is about life instead of death.

So many dead ideas walk among us like zombies. Some of these ideas include: Countries need to exercise power over one another; homeless people cause their own homelessness; and people should be paid what they are "worth." This latter zombie idea somehow ends up with some executives getting paid more every year than many people will earn in a lifetime, and other people's unemployment checks having a funny way of running out. Jesus' ideas are the opposite of dead. They are different. They unsettle us. They prioritize what we ignore, and they connect us to one another so that we won't use the word "other" as a term of exclusion. God loves our smallness and our very insignificance. God conceives a different kind of nation, a universal one based on God's love and mercy, one in which different kinds of humans do not despise themselves or others for being small or insignificant. This idea is such a reconception of how we usually imagine ourselves that it takes a lot of unpacking.

First of all, most of us are looking for a strong leader. No one else dare apply. However, God is the leader, not a mortal human. Any human that leads as though he or she were God is suspect. Leaders can be strong by making sure that they know they are not God. Leaders are stronger when they connect with the wider hope of a reconceived humanity, where all will be able to put their gifts on the table. Leaders are stronger when they hope for a larger, more diverse, more interconnected whole. Leaders are weaker when they primarily seek to protect their turf. Leaders are weaker when they separate and exclude groups from the community. Leaders are weaker when they rely on gossip or put someone else down to raise themselves up. Romans 15 invites us to welcome one another. It assures us that we don't need to have enemies. It reconceives notions about power in terms of power based upon encouragement, welcome, and living in harmony through Jesus Christ.

Secondly, the Gentiles and the Jews will be a part of the same great nation. People who are different will come together. The reconception of human society is strong. According to many early Jewish followers of Jesus, Jews and Gentiles were not meant to be together. It would be like me saying that a drug dealer and the president of a large bank should have lunch, or that a CEO should take a custodian to dinner, or that a 97-year-old woman in a nursing home should receive personal attention from the head of the corporation that runs the home. Paul appeals to Scripture and to his own respect for God's law in order to reconceive human society as God's people. Romans 15 is about more than nations. We are talking about a fundamental rearrangement of things, some of which we have to do ourselves.

Third, there is no big or small in this new nation of God's people. Instead, there is a rebirth of the very idea of a nation. Will this kind of nation come into constitutional being any time soon? Probably not. Christians live with the hope of this vision. Figuratively speaking, we are still on our way to Jews and Gentiles being one under God. It is God who leads us and who binds us together in Christ. Paul closes his description of this new nation, this new life in Christ, with a benediction: "May the God of hope fill you with all joy and peace in faith so that you overflow with hope by the power of the Holy Spirit" (15:13). The baby whose birth we will celebrate—

the promised branch from Jesse's root, God's gift of love, the One who will rule according to God's ways of love—embodies this hope.

How do you respond to the vision of people who are different from one another living together with mutual respect according to God's ways of mercy and justice? How can you live and practice this vision day by day?

FEAR, WATER, AND FIRE
MATTHEW 3:1-12

John the Baptist asked some of the religious leaders who came to be baptized, "Who warned you to escape from the angry judgment that is coming soon?" (verse 7). John is picking a fight with the religious status quo and declaring it counterfeit. With his admonition, he may be addressing fear in some of the religious leaders. When we reconceive the question, John might as well be asking, "Who told you to be afraid?" Many among these leaders were complicit with the authorities of Rome rather than to the vision of a social order according to God's will as expressed in the Law and through the prophets.

When we think of the reconceived question, we can be moved to the core of our injuries, miseducations, falls, and collapses. Once wounded, did we only predict more wounds? Or can a love powerful enough to change us also realign us? Who told us to be afraid? Then, who is telling us to remain afraid? Could we obtain permission to let us see something that is different from what we thought we would see? Can conception come to those of us who have lost our vision late in our careers? Or are we stuck in the same old same old of tired preconceptions? Can we break out? That is the question for the second week: Can we come out of the jail of our injuries and preconceptions long enough to imagine a new way, one that has love for the weak and the strong, the young and energetic along with the old and the tired? John makes a big promise, the kind that fits our longing. If you ever wanted renewal as much as you wanted to be excited—not burnt out but really lit—you will be a fan of John's big promises.

Interestingly, this text is a fuss about baptism. Baptism is often understood as the fundamental reorientation for a Christian. If a child is baptized, the child becomes a new member of the body of Christ. When an adult is baptized, they die to their old self and become a new person. They submerge in order to rise. John is saying that the kind of baptisms he does, just baptisms of water, are inferior to the kind that are to come. He says, "The one who is coming after me is stronger than I am. I'm not worthy to carry his sandals. He will baptize you with the Holy Spirit and with fire" (verse 11). Jesus will light people up in a way that John's water cannot.

If you have ever wanted renewal as much as you wanted a cup of water on a hot day, you understand what he is saying here. You see that renewal is a longing, and that people have longed for renewal for a long time. We want to be different. We don't want the same old, same old. But we don't know how to reconceive our lives and to move toward a new conception. Some people have lost their longing. They find hope too painful. For some people, it is uphill both ways. They don't just climb Mount Everest one day; they climb it every day. These are the people Jesus loves especially. These are the ones for whom he really wants renewal.

The rite of baptism offers renewal that is prefigured by a change of heart, the kind that keeps us from being afraid of hope to having a little hope. We experience some kind of turn, some kind of softening, some kind of deepening. We get ready to be baptized by fire. Often the turn is a turn toward some kind of tenderness. We learn to love something we didn't think we could love any more. The nest for hope is made in our hearts. Most congregations, including mine, could learn to love Jesus' people more—the ones who snore during service, whose feet hurt from waiting on tables, whose only life is a pack of beer after a long day of bosses and boredom. Often the turn comes when we become tender towards our wounds or the wounded among us.

Sometimes the turn towards tenderness comes from an abrupt change that happens to us, and we realize that even our ordinary longings are no longer on the table. Perhaps we get fired. Those pink slips really have a way of turning us around. In nearly forty years of active advocacy ministry, I have only been fired twice. The first time was for letting a chapter of the Gay Student Alliance use a room in the chapel. I was told that sinners are not allowed in the chapel. Because I believe that all people are sinners, I canceled Sunday services. They got the point and took me back. The second time was for raising too much money for a community-owned taxi company. We got put out of business, and I got fired. Why? Because a regulated industry like taxis in Connecticut must charge a profit. Imagine what would happen if other regulated industries didn't make a profit. The other reason for this firing was for asking a donor to give to something in the community. Lesson: Don't compete with your boss, especially for money.

Whether we get fired or not, or become tender or not, whether our longings are met or missed, most of us understand the difference between lavender and purple, between watery baptism and fire baptism, between same old, same old and excitement. Some of us have even used the words "This was a baptism by fire" before. During Advent, we have a little window

of time, like those little windows in the calendar. Each day we can reconceive ourselves and open ourselves to be baptized by the fire and Spirit of
Jesus Christ.

*What part of your life would you like to reconceive? What new conception might be
there for you? How might Jesus offer new fire for you or light your way?*

Sacrament: Finding the Holy in the Ordinary

Scriptures for Advent:
The Third Sunday
Isaiah 35:1-10
James 5:7-10
Matthew 11:2-11

We have come to the third week of Advent, which is going to surprise us with the holy. What is *the holy*? It is the ordinary perceived as sacred. God may be above and beyond, as far away and beautiful as the stars on a cold night; but God is also here now, as close as the baby's breath to a nursing mother.

One of the words we use for the holy perceived in the ordinary is the word *sacrament*. Often that word refers to bread and wine become body and blood or water become baptism. It can also mean the transformation of the daily into the eternal. In this third week, we are going to become sacramental. We are going to sleuth the holy in the ordinary and the eternal in the now, in the same way the best detectives use the smallest clues.

Larking, harking, barking, and snarking will stay with us. We will lark the paradox of a desert blooming. We will hark the sound of God as we wait for a bus. We will bark what we know to anyone who will listen, particularly to those whom Jesus calls the least of these. And our snark will always be present. We will remember how often we have disrespected the ordinary and been bored by it. A little confession can go a long way. Sacramental notions often take us in the most populist of directions. We patiently realize that the little things carry big meanings. In the dry desert, there is fertility. In the common act of patiently waiting, we can find the holy.

Isaiah 35:1-10 is full of astonishment. Deserts will bloom, the lame will walk, and the deaf will hear. Magnificent things will happen to those who are not used to magnificence. Harmony will return to those who are used to fighting. Gladness will come to those who thought their main objective was being right.

James 5:7-10 is about patience—the kind a farmer has after the seed is put in the ground. Patience is not just waiting for the bus; it is waiting for salvation. Waiting for the bus can be done as though we are waiting for salvation. That is what sacrament means. We find the holy in the ordinary. Instead of tapping our fingers and toes as we wait, we wait patiently and find ourselves filled with the powerful presence of God. We "practice" the presence of God in a sacrament.

Matthew 11:2-11 takes us again to John the Baptist. He is now in prison. He is still waiting patiently for the Messiah, but the apparent certainty about Jesus that he communicated in Matthew 3:1-15 is not clear in this account. John sends his disciples to Jesus with a question: "Are you the one who is to come, or should we look for another?" (verse 3). Jesus' enigmatic response beckons us to look again at the world around us.

THE WILDERNESS WILL BLOSSOM
ISAIAH 35:1-10

Isaiah 35:1-10 evokes the memories of God's people in the wilderness. The Book of Exodus says that in spite of the people's grumbling and disobedience, God was with them and provided for them (Exodus 15:24-25; 16:2-4; 17:1-7). Isaiah promises a journey home from exile that will be a new exodus through a well-watered desert that blooms and rejoices (35:1-2, 6-7).

Like the ancient Hebrews in the wilderness, Christians are used to fussing. We love being right. It is bread and butter to us. It is mother's milk. It is meat and potatoes. It is ordinary, not extraordinary. Fussing is what we do to prove that we are right. If we imagine this as a neighborhood, sacramental theology is on the block past being right. It is the experience of the powerful presence of God when we are grumbling and fussing, wrong or right, muddled or uninterested. Seeing God's presence involves hopeful waiting and trust in what God deems ordinary, the power of love. In this love, we see miracles. In the miracles, we are no longer right so much as we are connected to love. We see and experience God's presence.

Being right is no small thing, nor is fussing about being right. Many of us spend hours, days, and years getting our resumes right, reading the right books, learning the right arguments, getting the right grades for the right papers rightly written. Isaiah reminds us that life promises more than grumbling, complaining, fussing, and being right. Being right is not our destination. Instead, blossoming is our destination. Ordinary people can't always be right about everything, or at least not at the same time. Ordinary people instead can live flowering, that place on the next block after the fussing.

Why repeat that word, *ordinary*? Because sacraments find the holy in the ordinary, even in the ordinary that is less than our best selves. When we go to the block beyond being right, when we walk through our trivial natures, we find a deeper ordinary, a new normal, and a place beyond being right. It is like walking on Isaiah's highway (see verses 8-10). We can hear what Isaiah is saying as a sacramental appreciation of the universe. While we are fussing about the desert looking dry, the desert is actually blooming. The feeble look weak now, but we see them as they are becoming. The blind look blind now, but they also will see. The self-righteous part of us is just a stuck place. We can move through it. When we look sacramentally at just about anything, we see its hope and its destination, not just its present. We learn to wait and watch the flower grow, even though it takes forever to do so. We overcome ordinary human difficulty when we live in the assurance that we won't actually have to wait forever. It will just feel that way. When we have a hope of something good at the end—not something trivial or irritating or painful—our focus shifts from being right to being open. We still care about being right, but we don't care about it in an ultimate way. We don't go to the mat over being right. We go to the mat to perceive the desert blooming, the lame walking, the blind seeing. We sleuth the ordinary for its hope. In hopeful waiting, we find love all around us. In anxious action, we see the love slip away. Patience makes the difference between the two. Sometimes patience is just putting one foot in front of the other.

Being sacramental is being able to see the bloom in the desert. How can we mere mortals do that? Certainly, we can move out of the behavior of fight and flight into the behavior of tend and befriend. Are you in a fuss with someone you love? Back off for a while and consider why you loved them in the first place. Go into silence and solitude as sacrament and discover what you really want out of the fuss. If you want to be right, you probably are wrong. If you want to connect, you can find a way to do so. It will have to do with getting that "right" part of you out of the way of the connection.

Isaiah tells the people to be strong and without fear because God is coming to save (verses 3-4). How can we hear these words? There is no need to think of ourselves as weak. People so often think that love is weak. Just the opposite is true. What the world thinks of as weak is actually strong. Strength is sacramentally available in silence and solitude, in the ability to stand by, tending and befriending, as well as asserting and arguing. Do we feel scared in silence, sacrament, or solitude? Of course, we do! It was probably that original scare that drove us to the fight. We need to find out what we can't give up, and then don't give it up. But don't expect that we will find it by asserting it. We find it by tending and befriending our antagonists and ourselves. When we quietly say what we want, we have become a part of the desert in bloom. When we argue for it, our destination is a dry place. Did you hear the prophet say that we are to strengthen the weak hands and support the unsteady knees? If we face the scare, it will scare us less. There is glory in facing the scare, in tending and befriending it in ourselves, and in opening the space for it to be tended in others. When two frightened people meet and don't know how frightened they are of losing the other, sacrament is evaded. When two frightened people meet and acknowledge how weak and unsteady they are, sacrament is invoked.

Perhaps you have more social fusses in the way of your sacramental living. Are you in a fuss on a church committee or on the job? When we stop talking for a while, a long while, so long that people eventually ask us why we haven't said anything, we can tell them we were tending our trouble, tending it so deeply that we were looking for the promise in the pain. We had decided on listening rather than loading. Perhaps they will hear, and perhaps they will also learn to listen, to tend to the promise hidden in the pain. How else can we see the ordinary miracle of the deaf hearing, the lame walking, the blind seeing, or the mute singing (verses 5-6)? Our fussing, our grumbling, and our need to be right have not resulted in bloom or blossom. In Advent, we try another way. It is the way of God's love, perceived in the ordinary. It is acknowledging the strength of weakness. It is the way of God's love, astonishing us by a different practice, that of sacramentally standing by, alert to the blossoms coming out of the parched ground.

When did a desert bloom in your own life? When did something come to life that you thought was dead? What brought the change about? How did you experience God's presence and provision?

PATIENCE, PATIENCE
JAMES 5:7–10

The Book of James offers a variety of teachings about how to live while waiting for the coming of the Lord. The teachings are grounded in the wisdom and presence of God. Every gift comes from God and will produce fruit in our lives (1:5, 17-18; 3:17-18). It is in this presence of God emerging in our ordinary lives that we once again encounter a biblical call to sacramental living. We think and act out of our awareness of God's presence and practice of wisdom. This ground is holy ground! Holy ground that yields fruit! So, our Scripture moves over this sacramental ground to talk about patience as we "wait for the coming of the Lord" (verse 7). James 5:7-10 addresses courageous patience as well as grumbling and complaining.

If patience is such a good virtue, even bringing us to the feet of the sacramental, why is it so hard? Please permit me to be impish here. Sometimes, people put off many good things precisely because they are being patient. I don't respond well when judges tell me to be patient about justice or when a boss advocates patience for a raise. My own parents drove me crazy as I waited for Christmas. "Just be patient," they said. Even though I can appreciate impatience as a virtue as well as patience, in this Advent meditation on God's love, I think patience will win the day. You can't demand that God loves you. What you can do is refuse to grumble against God or others. You can experience love's reality over time, through friends, family, congregation, or pudding.

One good approach to the advice about patience in our own history is jazz music. Listen to Dave Brubeck's "Take Five." Then take five. Take five ways of seeking the sacramental in the ordinary. Take five when your tongue is flippantly open or angrily closed. One patient direction will probably work, even if the others fail. When they don't get you to your destination of the experience of God in ordinary time and life, take five more. Make them talk to each other, rising and falling, illumining and darkening, thinning and deepening.

James 5:9 gives us an extraordinary test of our patience. It says that we are "not to complain about each other." I wonder if this means that we can't use gossiping as a cheap means to connect with each other; or if it means we can't compete with each other by spreading bad news. You have seen the consequences of gossip. I'll never forget one of my Sunday school teachers who babysat for a new family within the church. They didn't negotiate what the price would be at the outset, so when the mother gave the babysitter the amount at the end of the night, it was much less than the sitter usually received. Instead of saying that it was less than she had expected, she said nothing. Not addressing difficult situations with each other—as in complaining face to face in hopes that reconciliation will prevail—is a snarky kind of despair. There is no lark in it, just snark. The next thing that happened was a public grumble. "Don't babysit for so-and-so because they are cheap." When that word went out in the congregation, without any direct hopeful reconciling conversation, the complaining became toxic. When the mother asked other Sunday school teachers to sit for her children, the answer was always no. The complaining had grown. Finally, someone told the mother why no one would babysit. The complaining broke her heart, shamed her in public, and caused her and her entire family to leave the church. The complaining had achieved a terrible victory. Complaining about each other is not only immoral, but it also has consequences. Sometimes the consequences can't be revoked. In this case, it led to exclusion. Maybe the Sunday school teacher couldn't assert her "rights" to more money right then. She could have thought it through and called the mother another day. She could have gone positive instead of negative in her direction and in her complaint. She could have connected.

Is there a sacramental way for speech? Yes, there is. It has to do with the active refusal of gossip. It is to replace the ordinary of gossip with the ordinary of connection. Every time someone tells you something about another person, even and especially if it is a way of "helping" you or "protecting" you, you can just smile with a sacrament in mind and suggest you really don't want to know what they are telling you. There is no need to jump on a high horse about it. Instead, you smile an ordinary smile. You refrain from listening. You quietly move into a deep patience about humanity, and there you rest. Whether you talk too much or too little, complaining about one another has no place in your hope to find love. It won't work. Talk when you want to and don't talk when you don't want to or when you know you shouldn't. Why not begin and end in patience and in hope?

Distance from God is worse than any cancer and has similar consequences. The person who learns patience is more likely to see God's presence, God's mercy, and God's compassion in the everyday and ordinary. The trick to learning patience is to be patient about it. Let it come when it comes. Instructions for sleuthing the sacramental in the ordinary might be similar to the instructions found on a box of chocolate pudding: Things need to have time to jell at their own pace. Imagine the ordinary, patiently awaited, having treasures within it. We don't need the fast, nasty connection of gossip. We need the slow growth of ordinary relationships in ordinary times. And, as James reminds us, we need the wisdom of God. We need to say with James, "The coming of the Lord is near" (verse 8).

What occasions in life cause you to be impatient? Where do you see a need to practice patience? How might your patience help you discover God's presence in your everyday life and relationships?

ARE YOU THE ONE?
MATTHEW 11:2–11

There is a sacramental rhythm to these ins and outs between Jesus and John that is grounded in the Isaiah prophecy. Both are denying their own power and locating it in healing, the kind that transforms lives. Both put down their own agency and align with the power of God as the force within them. Both self-efface and show an astonishing humility. John and his disciples were probably a little like us in their sleuth of the sacred. They imagined it grand and glorious while it was sitting right next to them in the suffering of ordinary people, a suffering hungering for change.

Earlier in Matthew 3, John seemed to point to Jesus as the Messiah (verses 11, 13). His confidence is not so certain in Matthew 11. He sends his disciples to Jesus to ask, "Are you the one who is to come, or should we look for another?" (verses 2-3). This text about John's question to Jesus— Are you the real thing?—reminds us of the main way Jesus credits himself. He never answers the question about whether or not he is the Messiah. Instead of answering, he goes for the evidence. Do you see healings? Do you see formerly blind people regain their sight? Do you see lame people able to move beyond where they were? Do you see motion in people no one thought could move? Do you see leprosy disappearing? Or in today's context, we might say, Do you see individuals with AIDS being healed? Do you see people who thought they could never hear again gaining or restoring their hearing? Do you see new life coming to people who thought they were dead? Do you see poor people being blamed for their poverty anymore? Do you see changes in the way the poor live?

The arc of the universe is bent towards transformative justice. When we see the holy in the ordinary person—who has been changed—then we will know the Messiah is near. John and Jesus come along and align with this hope. Sacramentally, I trust it. Their evidence is in the healing and changing of ordinary people. When handicaps change into assets, the Messiah is near. When the poor are no longer poor, we see the evidence.

In case you haven't noticed, many people want the poor to stay poor, the shut up to stay shut up, and the activists to become inactive. What sacrament means is that we join the holy in its action. Then we become the action that we have joined. We work with the Messiah in his project. Jesus is pretty crude in his defense of John. Who did you expect I would use, someone wearing soft clothes in kings' houses? No, I am going to use a prophet, a messenger, a wilderness man, someone more like you than not.

Am I willing to act with this promise, to go to jail for it, to speak it out loud? Or do I spend my days looking for a hotel room in the king's house, disregarding my wilderness? Jesus is signing up troops for his non-violent army. He is telling us that even one such as John can be a leader in the army of the ordinary becoming holy. Action filled with hope matters. The bent arc sometimes needs my weight hanging on it to keep it bent. That is not my virtue so much as my participation in God's great time, which is at hand. If I need to show—as in put skin in the game—I can also repent. John the Baptizer tested Jesus. Jesus "pinged." And his "ping" involves us.

We are part of the Messiah's work; we are his hands and feet. We are on that road set in the middle of a desert, even if its name is 42nd Street or the B15 bus. Whether by work, by patience, by patient work, or working patiently, the Messiah will come to earth and make the desert bloom. Sacramentally, our weight on the arc of justice may be as small as opening our mouth at the right time. We don't need to be jailed to be considered prophetic.

Think about John the Baptist sacramentally, as an ordinary man who carried the spirit. Like Jesus, he was a human; but he was a human who became a vessel for God. He was a wilderness prophet, not a king but a problem for kings. Herod of Antipas served up his head on a platter (Matthew 14:1-12; Mark 6:14-29). He was not a warrior. He was certainly not Jesus, although Jesus loved to hang out in the wilderness too. And he was certainly not Paul because John took too many risks and undid institutions instead of building them. It is interesting to think about how sacraments work: God uses what God decides to use, when God decides to use it. God's credentials aren't the point of the question. "Are you the one, or should we look for another?" The answer to that question is this: We need to look for ourselves and add our weight to the weight of the Messiah. That's when change comes; and when the change comes, the true Messiah is here.

When have you imagined that your time on earth might change something and make the world a better place? How do you think your actions can be part of God's work through Christ for wholeness, healing, and transformation?

GOD'S GIFT OF LOVE

Scavenging for Advent

Scriptures for Advent:
The Fourth Sunday
Isaiah 7:10-16
Romans 1:1-7
Matthew 1:18-25

We come to the fourth week in Advent, all wrapped up, all wound up, either ready or not ready for Christmas. Most of us are midway through our to-do lists, assuring others and ourselves that we are ready, whatever that means. I am going to dare to propose a meaning: We are ready for Christmas when our heart is hungry for the Messiah to be born. We are ready for Christmas the way a woman is ready to give birth when she is a week past her due date. We are ready for Christmas, even if the lists haven't even been made yet. We are ready to lark and mark, but sometimes we are so deep in snark that we don't know it. It is easy to get lost in Advent. Here the game is hide-and-seek. Can Advent find us? Can we find Advent? I say *yes* in my dared meaning: We can find Advent by scavenging it. Let me show you a way.

Some of us have started to say things like "I can't wait for Christmas to be over." Or, "My favorite foods are the leftovers." Or, "My favorite week is the week after Christmas." What is it about us that leads us to like the results more than the action, the after-party more than the party? I call this the scavenger in us. The scavenger finds the stuff that others miss. The scavenger is not impressed with bows and wrapping. The scavenger is not all wound up. She is unwinding into a long search for something divinely wonderful. And even better, he knows he is going to find it, even when the counter is full of unopened Christmas cards calling his name and the computer is full of beckoning e-mails. "Answer me. Answer me." We are ready for Christmas when we wake up in the day and know that something wonderful will appear out of nowhere, without a price tag, without a demand for attention.

Scavenging is a much more spiritual activity than anybody gives it credit. In this fourth week, we are going to learn about scavenging as a spiritual strategy. We are going to learn how magnificent it is that Jesus comes to free us. We don't have to work for him. We don't have to plan for him. We don't have to wrap him. He comes free, the way a good find on the side of the road comes free, without packaging. He comes just for us, almost as though God felt our hunger to be loved and met it.

The prophet Isaiah really puts it to the house of David. "Isn't it enough for you to be tiresome for people that you are also tiresome before my God?" (verse 13). Ouch. Not a pretty little sugarplum of a Christmas text is it? This also may be to be the reaction we have from the words of Paul to the Romans. In his introduction, he writes that he has been "set apart for the gospel" (Romans 1:1). What does it mean to be set apart? You don't really belong to those cards or those e-mails. You belong to something different. Then, in the Matthew text we are told about how the birth of Jesus happened. We heard about Joseph's dignity and his need to protect his pregnant fiance from shame. We are told that the Holy Spirit creates this child in Mary's womb. We see the angels are involved. The angels name the boy Emmanuel, God with us. All these things come to our befuddled Joseph in a scavenged dream, and he takes them all as true. In each of these texts we find meanings we didn't think were there. We scavenge from the part of ourselves that is set apart for God, even when weary. We scavenge from the set-apart self, even when we are just following dreams and the strange advice of angels about what to do next.

WORLD WEARY
ISAIAH 7:10-16

Christians find deep meaning in Isaiah 7:10-16, which contains the sign of Immanuel given by the prophet Isaiah to King Ahaz during the time of the Syro-Ephraimitc war. Ahaz is not at all eager to hear God's sign, probably because he has his own plans to align with Assyria in order to deal with the political upheaval.

The conversation does not go well. God tells Ahaz to wait for a sign. Ahaz, unbelieving, says, "I won't ask; I won't test the LORD" (verse 12). God is not pleased with the response and suggests that the way Ahaz has already wearied people will not wash. Addressing Ahaz as a representative of the whole house of David, Isaiah speaks about weariness. He says to Ahaz, "Hear then, O house of David! Is it too little for you to weary mortals, that you weary my God also?" (verse 13, NRSV). Without waiting for an answer, Isaiah goes on to say that the sign is coming, bidden or unbidden. A sign is coming in a child born of a virgin. We are told what the child will eat—butter and honey.

Then Ahaz hears the downside of the good news: Israel and Aram will be deserted, and Assyria will become a threat to Judah. I imagine Ahaz feels more than weary after this exchange. He is caught in his unbelief. He doesn't trust the visit of his Lord and gets a big promise, which he resists, only to discover that the land he loves will be devastated by Assyria.

Isaiah responds to Ahaz's unwillingness to be open to the sign from God by talking about human weariness and how it bores and bothers the divine. It is a sign to us as well. How can we weary one another and God? How dare we be weary in Advent? Will our weariness keep us from hearing God's sign to us? Isaiah's unminced words announce that the Messiah is nigh, right in the middle of the nation's squabbling and weariness.

One of the forms weariness takes this time of year, when the winter solstice has yet to arrive, is a hunger for the warmth and sun of spring. We stay under the covers longer because we know that it is cold outside. We stay under covers longer because we don't have anywhere truly compelling to go. In the spring, there is the sunshine to find, even if nothing else seems appealing. I know people who have spring weariness. I know people who have winter weariness too. Somehow the winter version is harder.

Ahaz's weariness is probably the winter kind, the kind that keeps your hopes under cover because you just can't dare trust that God has come to call or that Immanuel is nigh. His weariness is also the kind some know in spring, that depression that happens even while the sun is shining. We can snark at the consequences of Ahaz's disbelief. But we also have to look at the promises that we have passed. Many of us walk right by good stuff and don't even know what we have missed. It may not be the visitation of the Lord, telling us that Immanuel is coming and we may lose our land if we don't shape up. What we pass by may not be so consequential, either positively or negatively. This Scripture is a warning to pay attention, to learn to scavenge the spirit in our midst, to be less weary so that we can be more open whether it is summer or winter, Advent or Lent.

The winter version of weariness is especially hard on leaders. So many things have been promised, only to decay. Isn't it ironic that we cause other humans and God to become weary because we are weary, only to find that the weariness keeps us apart from that which would enliven us? Weariness is a terrible cycle. I remember someone saying to me that she just didn't know how tired she was. I heard another person say that slaves used to say they were tired today and tomorrow and down into the next century. How do we jump out of the cycle of fatigue so that we are not forced to pass by what is good and right in front of us?

I like to scavenge as a spiritual practice because it keeps me off the cycle of decay and fatigue. I see what can blossom in what is dead or forsaken or left behind. Ahaz faced the devastation and loss of his land because he couldn't hang on in hope or alertness. Advent scavengers hang on in hope and alertness.

One time in Florida, in that great week after Christmas, I took all the poinsettias that had gone bad from church after church and put them in the garden at our church. You would not believe what happened. They revived, and no one has been able to stop their thriving. We also added the Easter lilies, using the same ecclesiastical dumpster scavenging in the spring. Same resurrection. They bloomed and re-bloomed and re-bloomed some more. The Women's Fellowship finally had a meeting about the reproducing Easter lilies and poinsettias. Something had to be done to keep these scavengers from taking over the entire church's garden. Needless to say, I was amused; and amusement is one of the great gifts of scavenging. Odd things happen, and you enjoy them. Amusement is also one of the best antidotes to weariness. It lifts us up.

Even here in New York City, people throw planted pot after pot out on the street. I carry them home. They make the dirt for my tiny back- and front-yard gardens, where the morning glories thrive. People stop to take pictures of the glories, as they are so beautiful in the summer. I scavenge their seeds too, thus getting five different colors blending deep into the fall.

This fourth week of Advent is not an easy time to be a dirt scavenger. Things are still in seasonal bloom. But by next week, the scavenging of the city streets will become magnificent, and the throwaways won't just be dirt. Think couches, coats, blenders, printers. Advent is anticipation of a scavenger's holiday, as well as that week after.

If only Ahaz had hung onto what God was trying to tell him! Imagine what he might have found. He might have found the promise of the Messiah. Instead, he resisted it, causing peril on his land and people. Could he have been taught instead to scavenge in the middle of his fearful and wearying ways? Or did God have to hit him upside the head? What about you and me? What are we passing by right now?

When have you been too weary to see signs of God's promise in your life? How might recognizing Immanuel or God with Us offer hope? How can "scavenging" for meaning become a spiritual discipline for you during such times?

SET APART
ROMANS 1:1-7

Our epistle reading for this fourth Sunday is a salutation common in Greco–Roman letters during Paul's time. What could such a greeting offer to us as we scavenge for meaning during this Advent season? Paul uses it to set a rich theological ground for what it means to be a follower of Jesus Christ. We could call it a mini-sermon or a mini-gospel about God's grace and about our call "to be God's people" (verse 7), even though we may be weary of the season and tired of waiting for Christmas! Even though we hurt. Even though we feel like losers. Even though we feel lost.

When Paul tells the Romans that they are "set apart," we get good advice about how to scavenge our situation. We are not so much *lost* in our weariness and waiting as we are *set aside*, like other apparently useless things, put out on the curb, awaiting repurposing. When we remember that we are *set apart* as those who belong to Jesus Christ, our energy returns, and the people will follow. When we think of Christmas readiness, we know we are ready to stand with the outsiders, outside. When we think of Easter, the destination of Christmas, we realize that it also has less to do with trumpets than it has to do with a couple of lost and confused women holding onto one another on an early morning. In each case, the shepherds and the women are scavenging a meaning that will startle the world. Even in our weariness and in our waiting, we are set apart to repair the breaches and cling to each other in the precious predawn of hope. We wait with a wonder about whether we will ever have to stop wondering. We keep a lookout for what might be thrown away or tossed aside.

One breach between who we are and the promise of the Advent season is the awful hate that is flourishing—hate against lesbian, gay, transgender, and bisexual individuals, Muslims, immigrants, people who are different, and people we perceive as threats because they are different. Hate flourishes because institutions stay in denial instead of daring the dawn. We are here to repair the breach and end the denial. We do so with people who, like discarded poinsettias and Easter lilies, are set so far aside that their unemployment checks ran out spiritually and materially a long time ago. Who are our people here? Those who rest beside the weary road. Those who bend down and are bent down. Those crushed by life's weary road. To them we scavenge and sing a carol from our set-aside place. We are here to raise up the promise of Advent, to be tender with each other in grief. The rest will follow. We may even find a purpose alongside the weary road.

We scavenge our spirits in a world that does not support, recognize, or obey them. Are we ready for Christmas from here? Yes, indeed. We are more than ready. We are hungry. We are alert. Our eyes are peeled. We stand on tiptoes, ready for our next purpose. One more matter should come on the plate of the set-aside spiritual scavenger, who is so ready for Christmas that he can't sleep, like a child alert for the Christmas presents usually is. This scavenger is alert for the Christmas *presence*, not the *presents*, although they are fun too. I'm going to call that matter "generational."

Let me try to scavenge some meaning from the generational shift. I remember when my parents first saw me wearing blue jeans. They were horrified. Now I notice that many people wear their baseball hats backwards. I wonder why they don't wear them the right way, which is the way we wore them in my day. Back in the day, I tell them, people wore their baseball hats the right way. I meet people who don't approve of social media sites or of the underwear that young women wear. Have they really forgotten how they broke their own parents' hearts right in front of the neighbors?

Generational misunderstandings are universal and maybe even harmless. We seem to need to justify ourselves. One of the ways we do it is by wearing what our parents didn't and wearing them the way our parents didn't as well. Elders deserve respect because they are elders. Youth only lose when they forget to respect the old, just as the old only lose if they don't find out what younger people are thinking under their baseball caps. The best thing we have learned in my congregation—which is getting younger—is not to mention age very much. The way we treat each other as people is what matters. Customs don't. People do.

What meaning does the generational shift have to the scavengers who know they are set aside? It means that we don't hang onto the main road or the main line. Instead, we take the side roads and the byways and get back in touch with our inner shepherd, our need to go and see what God reveals (Luke 2:15). We get happy and real on the sideline. I have hope for younger people and older people who know what it means to love a person for who they are and learn to avoid the shallow sneers.

In today's world, too many people do not have security that is social. I eagerly await "social security" for all! Instead, we feel set aside. We feel like we have to dig, scavenge, and hunt for meaning, a meaning that we don't really think is there. What Advent might re-teach us (because we do already know) is that the best place for a Jesus person is out in the field, keeping watch over all the flocks, the lambs and the sheep. From there, we scavenge our spirits and stop worrying about being set aside. We remember that we are "set apart for God's good news" (verse 1) and that we are "dearly loved by God and called to be God's people" (verse 7).

What breaches do you see between who you are and the promise of Advent? What does it mean to you to be "set aside"? to be "set apart"?

LISTENING TO THE DREAM
MATTHEW 1:18–25

Matthew's account of the birth of Jesus shows Joseph as a righteous man who scavenges a shameful situation and finds a compassionate way out. Mary, his betrothed, is pregnant; and he is not the father. The law called for public trial and execution (Deuteronomy 22:23-27). Joseph chooses a more compassionate way. He does not want her to be humiliated and chooses to quietly call off their engagement. He has stepped off the main road and chosen a sideroad. Then he has a dream that takes him off the side road and onto a backroad! And in so doing, he offers a lesson to all of us who step onto sideroads and backroads as we seek clarity in cluttered situations. He listens to the dream given to him in his scavenging, the dream that revealed the promise of God, the dream that revealed the purpose and ministry of the child, the dream that revealed the child's name, Emmanuel, God with us, Jesus, *yeshua'* which means "to save." Joseph takes the unconventional route, the backroad. He takes Mary as his wife. When the child is born, he continues to heed the dream and names the child Jesus.

Spiritual scavengers manage their weariness and cluttered lives by learning to enjoy the side roads, the back roads, the long way home. We expect that we will find useful things in the garbage. We expect that God will come in a new and unusual way, and that many will miss God's coming. We also imagine that we might miss the glory of Advent because we are so busy with our obligations on the counter and in the computer. We will have become the kind of people who imagine that nothing good can come out of Nazareth, especially from the likes of Mary and Joseph, pregnant out of wedlock.

We are ready for the news of Christmas when we have decided that scavenging is a good thing, a noble thing, not a thing to be frowned upon. Many people look down on things that are secondhand, used, or "found." They will never be ready for Christmas. They will never understand what Joseph heard from the angels and trusted: Your son, who mystifies you, will be born by your wife, who mystifies you, and his name will be Emmanuel, God with us. Let me be confessional as a way of showing how hard it is to be truly Christian, to truly follow and find the meaning of Jesus. That meaning is grace, not obligation. It is freedom, not bondage. It is joy, not sorrow. It is sourced in simple people, not in fancy people. It comes to us by trust, not by trying.

I finally had my first sabbatical after 38 years of active ministry. I knew freedom would make me nervous. When you define yourself by your work, and then you don't work for a while, "whoops" becomes your middle name. Once you are on sabbatical, you lose all your excuses. Your peace is no longer a problem of the schedule or of human sorrow. You are separated from the schedule and from the sorrow, intentionally, and contractually. You are excused from it and excused from your excuses. Sabbatical separates the skin from the onion. It privileges the inner life over the outer life, the being over the doing, and the reflection over the action. It is a guarantee that you can find peace. But what if you don't? What if you hear the angels sing their song and just don't finally trust it? That is my confession. I didn't trust the angel's song the way Joseph did.

When I started this excuse-free time of peace and grace, I admit the air was out of my tires. I knew I would need a pump in order to return to hard work and useful things. The pump of grace would allow me to face the grief of the failure of action in parts of my life. If I just worked harder, would these failures not decrease? How dare I leave my congregation when so many of them were either so overworked or so underworked? Sabbatical would allow me to face the grief of action, and how action often doesn't do what it promises to do. Action promises to achieve justice, but sometimes it does not succeed. How could I help but hope that the pump of grace would achieve what action hadn't? How could I trust the angels' song or even let it come to me in a dream, knowing that I never really took that sabbatical that was so graciously given to me? I took it.

Sabbatical faces straight into the terror of grace. I swam. I sat. I read. I listened to endless public radio. I went whale watching. I also found myself compulsively decluttering areas of my house, like desks, calendars, and kitchen cabinets. The word *clutter* comes from the Middle English word *clotter* and means "stuck energy" or "coagulation." *Decluttering* is a verb well associated with sabbatical. We get rid of things we do not use or love, e-mails and appointments, too many things in too small a space. We lay out our clothes. We either finish unfinished projects or abandon them. We no longer have good excuses for an untidy or disorganized desk. But even the decluttering gets in the way of the angel song. Listening to the dream is Joseph's way, the backroad way. Listening to the dream is where we rest beside the road. When we rest and listen there, we scavenge the Spirit's meaning. It will not come to us the way we imagine it will come. It will, however, come. We stay alert to find it.

What situations in your life need to be decluttered? How might you find a way to rest beside a weary road and listen to God's dream for you?

ℒove Is Born

Scriptures for Advent:
Christmas
Isaiah 9:2-7
Titus 2:11-14
Luke 2:1-20

Finally we are here. The stillness is coming. You can sniff it out the way a good snowstorm announces itself by a unique smell in the cold air or by the excitement right before lunch is ordered. You know "it" will soon be over for another year, and you hope it will and that it won't at the same time. Anticipation and expectancy are both high and nigh. The pulse quickens, and sometimes it is not just from the high blood pressure brought on by the stress of the season. Sometimes it quickens as promise received, hope realized, love experienced.

In this last week, the one long awaited, I want to talk about how love can be real in us, from us and for us. I want to hark love, mark love, and snark what we think might be love but is not. Love is something most of us want so much that we have learned how to be desperate for it. We look for love in all the wrong places, in pleasing others or displeasing them, in obeying the boss's orders or defying them, in calling negative attention to ourselves, and in sometimes hurting ourselves to get the attention we covet. If you have never self-sabotaged on the way to finding the love you covet, stop reading now. If you have, do continue.

Christmas is the experience of love, the holy arriving in the ordinary, the holly arriving to announce the holy. God makes a choice at Christmas. God chooses to come as a baby. Not a king, but a baby. We celebrate the Incarnation, Christ in the flesh. Earth is kissed by heaven, time is kissed by eternity, body and soul embrace in a great incarnational fiesta. God hauls eternity and heaven into time and earth.

Something shifts inside us, not outside us. Something new is happening in the way we experience love. It is a soft experience, not a tough experience. It is a turn in the corner, a decision to go away and not look for love in all the wrong places; but instead look for it in some of the right ones. The right place is that wistful, whimsical experience of the incarnation: God loves us. God is nigh. God has come gently to us, so as not to scare us.

God loves us. It doesn't matter any longer who else does or doesn't. It doesn't matter what we make happen as entrepreneurs in a new and scary world, one that offers less and less love and more and more obligation, turn by turn, day by day, tick of the clock by tick of the clock. What matters is what we know has already happened, making us strong enough on the inside to manage any external difficulty. We become dreamers who love from a source of power we didn't think we had. We are so full of grace that we love in ways we didn't know we could. As Christmas comes and becomes one holy night, we see all the other days and nights of yore in a new light.

Yes, parents, children, or former partners inexpertly loved us. Our jobs turned into jobs, not vocations; and no one seemed to care. We did not find a calling in our volunteer lives or a working environment where our gifts were used and evoked. We were also unloved on the subway or in that commute which just seemed to take longer and longer, leaving us less able to become our best selves by the mile per gallon. And no, that doesn't matter as much as God's decision to let the Word become flesh and dwell among us. When God comes nigh to love us, every now and then at Christmas, we experience that love. We melt. We move into the new being God has offered in Jesus' love. Christians see in Isaiah 9:2-7 the image of this love as light. As we turn toward the light of love in the birth of the child, we realize that we may not be able to change circumstances; but we can engage them with the confidence and power of God's love. Titus 2:11-14 remind us that God's grace empowers us to live God's way of love. The story of Jesus' birth in Luke 2:1-20 invites us to sing the season's carols with joy and praise.

TURN TOWARD THE LIGHT
ISAIAH 9:2-7

While Isaiah 9:2-7 is probably a coronation oracle celebrating a new king, Christians have traditionally viewed this Scripture as a description of the ideal messianic king and see Isaiah's vision fulfilled in Jesus Christ. The passage begins with the images of darkness and light, and includes the beloved names "Wonderful Counselor, Mighty God, Eternal Father, Prince of Peace," all of which point to the divine nature of the child who has been born for us (verse 6).

"The people walking in darkness have seen a great light" (verse 2). These words offered hope to the people of Judah during a time of great political turmoil and war. How can we hear them? We have lived in darkness by looking for love in all the wrong places—in our appearance, our success, our ability to give to others. When we have stopped looking to receive love because of our accomplishments, we have turned toward the light. When we see God's long-promised light in the baby Jesus, we see that we are loved by God. We begin to turn around, to change our ways. We no longer stare at the darkness because we love the light.

And what can that light look like in our lives? What vision does it offer to us? When we know we are loved, we no longer live in a time famine. Everything ordinary becomes holy to us. We reconceive ourselves and each other; and through the power and grace of God, love just slips out of us like water cascading its power down through the waterfall. We see glory in what others throw away and find what we need wherever we are. We scavenge the spirit sacramentally. Others may not see it, but it is right there in the manger blessed by birth or in the shepherds reawakened to find joy in their sheep and in the stars. Because we know God loves us, we love extravagantly. We no longer worry about whether someone deserves to be loved or not. Instead, we see people on the move, whom God also loves. We don't see a worthy underwater homeowner who deserves just treatment by the banks as compared to an unworthy one who overspent. Each person is loved by God the way all of us are loved by God, in a place beyond our self-righteous understandings of justice. Christmas comes into our lives, not just to our calendars.

The light in the darkness gives us what I like to call "soul spine." We aren't weak of spine but strong of spine. We are no longer puppets on another's string, dancing to the wrong drummer's beat because we misbelieve that they might love us if we do what they tell us to do. Now, we dance on our own string. We listen each other's souls into being. Because we have seen the light, we pull each other out of darkness.

Because we know that God loves us, we can become prophetic like Isaiah. We also become more capable of taking on the world's pain. It still dismays us but not in a hopeless way. We have hope in God and in our own ability to love through the power of God.

During Christmas two years ago, at a spa around the corner from where I live in New York City, a manicurist had to go to the bathroom. She had been washing people's feet for what she described as 12 straight hours. The owner of the shop said she could not go, as there were more clients and more feet. She refused the refusal. As she walked out of the shop that night, six other foot washers walked out with her. Of course, they were fired too. Later, through sobs on a phone call, she told us her story, begged for help, but then she disappeared. She wanted help she could not receive, for reasons I'll never know. Sometimes, she said, we can't receive the help we need because we are so afraid of the boss. We looked for the workers; but we could never find them, not through the Domestic Workers' Alliance, the Chinese Workers' Alliance, or several personal contacts. We never saw them again. Why were we looking? Because of Jesus. Because of Christmas. Because we know a God who has said goodbye to the darkness on behalf of the light loves us.

Knowing that God loves us allows us to search for people we can't find—even people who are so scared that they disappear into the streets of a big mean city. We are not afraid of our failure, but we are afraid *not* to give out our love. We are certain that love will prevail and that the unjust boss will not. Prophets don't become certain or convinced overnight. Nor does the darkness cease to try to invade the light. There is no "right" way to spread love around in my manicure episode. When we know we are loved, we go as far as we can. We relax in our failure but not in our love.

I no longer go to that salon around the corner. After my Christmas appointment that year, I was no longer welcome. I don't like women bowing down in front of me in the first place, but I do like supporting their growing businesses. I also enjoy their attention to my feet. I can't stop thinking about Jesus who washed feet and understood that the disciples didn't understand. Their quandary is mine. Just because you can't fix something or make it right doesn't mean that you can't love. Love is not about success and failure. Love is about love. We act without forcing; we love without fear. Prophetic love is often understood as naïve. Jesus' kindness is often mistaken for weakness. Humility is one thing, but bowing down is another. When we know we are loved, we aren't afraid to connect to the pain, our own or that of others. We are the people who have walked in darkness and may walk there again. But finally, for sure, we see a great light.

What does it mean to you to hear the words "the people who walked in darkness have seen a great light"? How does Christmas offer light in your darkness? How does it inspire you to love without fear, even when you may not be able to see that your love makes a difference?

SELF-CONTROL, GRACE, AND LOVE
TITUS 2:11–14

This lesson from Titus on God's grace follows a section that offers a list of instructions for commendable behaviors for those who follow Christ.

The list sounds a little like something a schoolmarm might write; however, it is also wise in its input. It wants members of the community of believers to practice self-control, which is a worthy goal. Our reading in Titus 2:11-14 provides the reason as well as the source of our capacity to behave in ways that are "self-controlled, upright, and godly" (verse 12, NRSV): God's grace and salvation born to us through Jesus Christ.

Most of us don't practice self-control because we aren't fueled to do so. We would have controlled ourselves if we could have. But since we can't, we didn't. The "woulda coulda" excuse is a great one. It works when our children tell us they didn't like the way we raised them or our best friends tell us why they had to betray us. We often spend considerable time working to achieve power and fame before we understand that love is their foundation. Power is good, if used in love. Fame is good, if used in love. Parents are good, if they truly love their children. We don't force consequences when we truly love. We love because we are loved. We love to love. If it is a legitimate goal to be self-disciplined, how do we get there without the bypasses, the excuses, the detours to distorted perceptions of power and fame? God's love breaks in. Love is the path.

One sneaky way power replaces love comes in what I call "do-gooders." The difference between a virtuous act and one that is not has to do with whether its source is love. Some acts of goodness come from that empty place in us, where we are practicing self-control to gain more power. We do good to get power or approval instead of doing good on behalf of love. When we feel unloved and powerless, the excuses flood in. Again, we would do good if we could, but we can't so we don't. Instead of focusing on our own need for love and experiencing the Christmas reality of the Incarnation, we love others in order to justify ourselves. We stay in the host position at the coffee hour but never understand how desperate we are for a cup ourselves. People who know the Christmas love born to us in Jesus Christ know that we are both guests and hosts at the great table of God. First, God loves us. That is our power. Then we love. That's it.

I'll never forget a night in Riverhead, New York, when I was pastor there. It was 4 P.M. on a cold Christmas Eve and an inebriated farmer rolled his truck up onto our front lawn and dumped a full load of turnips. "I want to help the pooooorrrr," he mumbled. We had to rush to get volunteers to put the dusty and dirty turnips into the cellar so people wouldn't trip over them on their way into the services. We didn't know what else to do with them. There they stayed till after the holiday, when an odor came through the church building. It was the smell of rotting turnips, something you rarely have the chance to experience on such a large scale. That's when the idea for the turnip cook-off developed. Anyone could come to the church, haul some turnips out of the basement and create a turnip dish. They also had to haul out a few smelly ones and throw them into the compost. On

January 15, we would have a big turnip cook-off, and the winner would receive a turnip-themed prize. The cookbook we finally published featured many dishes, including turnip cake, turnip casserole, baked turnips, fried turnips, stewed turnips, as well as turnips with garlic, cabbage, apples, and poppy seeds. The winning entry was my husband's "turnip fries." News 12 Long Island covered the event; and all of us had a good time. No one had to be the host or the guest. Everyone was welcome to participate. I personally explained to the farmer that he had a good idea that had gone bad; and that next time he dumped a load of turnips on our front lawn, I was going to have him arrested. I understand how his self-control was trying to assert itself on behalf of goodness. I even knew that all he had were the turnips. In theory, his act was virtuous. In practice, it was ridiculous. Such is the way of much of our do-gooding. I am reminded of all the canned goods that went to the Rockaways after Superstorm Sandy. People were donating cans to people who no longer had cupboards.

What could be different? We could remember what Titus says: "The grace of God has appeared, bringing salvation to all people" (verse 11). We could experience how much God loves us and not do desperate things like throwing turnips on a church lawn as a way to give. We could experience how much God loves us and learn to forgive that part of us that brings the wrong gifts at the wrong time to the wrong place. Then we could have fun. A cook-off of our mistakes almost always works.

What feelings or thoughts do you have about the call to "live lives that are self-controlled, upright, and godly"? How do God's grace, love, and salvation make a difference in your efforts toward self-control?

CAROL YOUR WAY TO PEACE
Luke 2:1–20

So here comes the full deal, the whole story. Mary has delivered the child. Pregnancy is over. The mystery is solved: A baby is born. Just a baby. And the takeaway is in the words of the angels to the shepherds, "Don't be afraid! Look!" (verse 10). What happens to us when we know God loves us, gently and carefully? We are no longer afraid. We look. We are preoccupied with grace and joy and love.

I don't know about you, but I am attached to Christmas carols. Say the words, "Joy of Heaven to earth come down," "Lo, the days are hastening on," or "Ye besides life's weary road," and my eyes moisten. Call me sentimental. The words in the Christmas carols are loving; it's almost like getting non-stop Valentine's cards from people you didn't think liked you at all. There is a big surprise in God's love. In this season, humility is exalted. The crooked are finished. Even we, whose intestines are all tied up in knots and who wouldn't know peace if it knocked on our doors, even we are straightened out. Silent night will become holy night, and all will be calm and all will be bright; that is what God is showing us as Advent begins. The little town of Bethlehem is lying in stillness, away from the manger; and joy is showing its route to the world in a baby king. Stars get brighter. Angels sing. The faithful all come. Hearts open to prepare the child's room. We see a rose blooming and find ourselves with nothing else to say but "Lo." Heralded angels sing, even in the bleakest mid-winter. Emmanuel comes. Captive Israel is ransomed. Bells jingle. Santa Claus comes to town. No wonder our eyes become moist with inner change.

The reason is that the emptiness of earth is filled with the glory of heaven. The crooked becomes straight, as we turn around. You may have to change your path to get on the path. You may have to be abnormal to be normal. You may have to love the material to not be materialistic. You may have to trust the small to live large. You may have to become better acquainted with vulnerability in order to be safe or saved. You may have to have less power in order to have more power. These are the unique Christian messages of Advent and what make the Christian religion still so pregnant with promise.

If the starting point is love and knowing we are loved, praise is the ending point. It is no accident that "Joy to the World" is the final hymn in most Christmas services. Or that "O Come all ye Faithful" is the big opener. Praise is the purpose of Christmas. If we miss its joy, we miss Christmas. If we find its joy, we find Christmas.

My friend has a sign on her refrigerator that reads, "It's not going to happen that way." She is preparing herself for a day and a life of surprises. She is grooming her "To-Don't" list. If we want to get the energy in our hands and the love deep in our hearts—the energy to clap or touch or wiggle, to be a guest in a great universe—we probably need to change our direction. Do less, plan less, and be more. Instead of working harder, we might work easier. We could skip out of the meeting as though we had an important call. Maybe it is coming from the Spirit. Take a "well" day. Get the Christmas cards out in July. Refuse to let Christmas turn your hands limp. Let Christmas clap your heart, wiggle your toes, and reach out to your friends.

So many of us say we "just don't have time." Even when doing something that makes us feel good, some of us can become pinched and hit ourselves with a stick on the way to pleasure or joy. "Punishmentalism" runs deep, and its objective is shame, that powerful fear that we are unworthy of connection. Christmas is the opposite. It is the permission to love because we have found out that we are loved. To erupt into praise at Christmas, we have to get strong pliers gripped tenderly and firmly onto punishmentalism; and we have to lift it out of our hearts.

Too many of us are looking for a bargain when a luxury is nigh. This Christmas would be a great time to notice what we have already seen. What we have already seen is that when leaders get too large, they revert to a brutal and brutalizing smallness. Too many presents under the tree are oppressive. "Don't get me anything," we lie to each other. "I already have too much." A parent who can be enchanted by a child, a lover who can be enchanted by a lover, a human who has a sense of being in charge—these are the presents we need to give and receive. What we have already seen is the failure of the Caesars and of our own material excess to provide a future for the children of the world. What we have already seen, if we would only look, is that big is usually too big and small can be tender and beautiful.

"Don't be afraid! Look! I bring good news to you—wonderful, joyous news for all people" (verse 10). Maybe our Christmas gift to each other can be to look, to notice what we have already seen. Notice this: We are loved. May that noticing, those pliers, that turn of heart and mind become praise for the gift of love born in the baby Jesus. May it be the kind of praise that meanness just can't survive. "Glory to God in heaven, and on earth peace" (verse 14).

What is the "good news" of Christmas for you? How might you sing praise to God?

LEADER GUIDE

HOW TO LEAD THIS STUDY

GOD'S GIFT OF LOVE invites adults to explore and reflect upon the Revised Common Lectionary Bible readings for the season of Advent. This Advent study is rooted in the texts for Year A of the three-year lectionary cycle of readings. Each week you will find readings from the Old Testament, the Epistles, and a Gospel. "How to Lead This Study" guides you in setting up and leading the study. You'll discover tips for preparing for each week's session, as well as ideas about how to successfully lead a Bible study, even if you have never led one before. Although the Revised Common Lectionary designates a psalm or words of praise for each week, they are generally not discussed in the main content. These additional Scriptures are, however, listed here for your convenience. "How to Lead This Study" offers some historical and theological information about the season of Advent and suggests ways that people now and in different times and places have observed this sacred time. In addition, you will find prayers and a selection of hymns appropriate for each week's session.

About Advent

Advent is the first season in the twelve-month cycle of seasons in the church known as the liturgical year. Advent is from a Latin word that means "coming." This definition is fitting, for during the season of Advent we await the coming of Christ. We look in two directions for this coming: backward in time to recall the birth of Jesus Christ in Bethlehem and forward as we anticipate his return. In Western churches, the season begins four weeks prior to Christmas on the Sunday closest to November 30th and ends on Christmas Eve. Altars have traditionally been adorned in purple, the color of royalty that reminds us of Christ's sovereignty. Purple is also associated with penitence, which is appropriate for this season because historically Advent, like Lent, has been a time to reflect and repent. More recently, blue has been favored in many churches because of its association with Mary, who artists often depict wearing blue. Just as Mary waited for the birth of her holy Child, so the church eagerly awaits his coming.

Advent is a time of preparation. However, some churches rush headlong into Christmas, skipping over this important time to get ready. Even on the first week of Advent, Christmas carols ring out. Nativity scenes feature the Magi, whose arrival is celebrated on January 6th, which is Epiphany. On the church calendar, the Christmas season begins with the birth of Jesus and ends with Epiphany. Although the secular world may push us toward Christmas, in the church we take the time to prepare ourselves for Christ's coming and coming again.

Advent has the potential to form and transform us if we allow that to happen. As we wait expectantly for the One God called Son, we bump up against the realities of the world with all its suffering, injustice, and hostility. Yet if we consider the scriptural promises of this season, we know that God is at work among us and within us to change not only ourselves but also the world. We live in the space between the first and second coming of Christ. God's realm has broken in upon us with Jesus' birth; it will appear in its fullness when he returns. In the interim, we live as Advent people who keep alert and constantly prepare for his coming.

Ways to Celebrate Advent

The season of Advent provides time for us to get ready for the coming— and coming again—of our Lord Jesus Christ. During this season of preparation, many people attend special study groups, just as you are doing, to discover what the Savior's coming is all about and what he means in their lives. People use Advent wreaths and Advent calendars as two means of personal spiritual growth. Another way to celebrate the season, setting up an angel tree, involves sharing resources with those in need.

ADVENT WREATHS: Many sanctuaries, Sunday school rooms, and homes are adorned with Advent wreaths. Scholars believe these wreaths were first used in northern Europe, and the traditions have varied; but by the sixteenth century, the wreath had taken on the form that we recognize today. The roundness of the wreath and the evergreens used to create it symbolize life. Traditionally, three purple candles are lit on the first, second, and fourth Sundays. A rose-colored candle, symbolizing joy, is lit on the third Sunday. More recently, blue candles are used for all four weeks. Some wreaths include a center white candle, which is lit late on Christmas Eve to symbolize Christ.

ADVENT CALENDARS: Originating in Germany in the late 1800's, Advent calendars provide a way to count down the days until Christmas, beginning on December 1. The calendar includes twenty-four small windows, and each window hides a picture. Although early calendars used images from the Old Testament, contemporary ones frequently display items appealing to children, such as teddy bears or candy.

ANGEL TREES: Some churches and other organizations decorate trees using angels, which are often made of construction paper. Listed on the angels are items that an individual or family in need would like to have for Christmas. Generally these lists include food, clothing (with sizes and colors indicated), and toys. Social-services agencies or schools usually provide lists. Those who choose to participate select an angel, purchase the requested items, and return them by the date specified on the angel. Some organizations ask that the gifts be wrapped; others prefer to wrap all gifts in a central location. Either way, gifts need to be marked using the number or code shown on the angel. A group of helpers delivers the gifts, usually on December 23rd or 24th.

Organize an Advent Study Group

Advent is an especially busy time of year for most people. Yet, it is also a time when Christians yearn to deepen their relationship with Christ. Study groups are an excellent way to enable people to delve deeper into the Bible and to reach out in friendship to others. Established groups—Sunday school classes, current Bible study groups, men's or women's groups—may choose to focus on Advent. Also consider forming a new group for this five-week Advent study. By advertising the study in local media, you can open wide the doors of the church to include those from other congregations—or no congregation at all.

When you, in conjunction with the pastor and church education team, have determined the shape of the group, decide when and where they can meet. An established group would most likely continue to meet in its regular space and time. A new group will have to be scheduled so as not to conflict with other activities that potential participants would likely attend, such as choir rehearsal. Evening meetings are more likely to pull in individuals who are still working, whereas daytime meetings may be more attractive to older adults who choose not to be out after dark, full-time parents, and perhaps college students. The time of the meeting will suggest whether refreshments are needed. A Saturday morning is a good time to offer a continental breakfast. A noon meeting could include the invitation to bring a bag lunch. An evening meeting might include some light snacks and beverages.

The learning space should be large enough for the group you anticipate. A Sunday school room with tables would be ideal. Since many churches conserve energy by regulating individual room temperatures, request that the room be properly heated by the time the participants arrive and remain so during the meeting time. Make sure that a small worship table and large writing surface, such as an easel with large sheets of paper and markers, a markerboard with markers, or a blackboard with chalk will be in the room. Have a separate space available and a designated worker to provide childcare.

Decide whether you want to hold a preregistration. Whether you do or not, be sure to order enough copies of GOD'S GIFT OF LOVE so that each participant has the study book. The church will need to determine how much to charge participants or whether to underwrite the cost and announce that the study is free.

Prepare for the Sessions

Leading a Bible study is a sacred privilege. Before you begin the "nuts and bolts" work, pray for the Holy Spirit to guide you and the participants as you encounter each week's Bible passages. Try reading each Scripture devotionally by asking God to speak to your heart through a word or phrase that grabs your attention. Meditate on whatever you are shown and allow this idea to shape your own spiritual growth.

Read the Scriptures and Bible Background for each week's lesson to understand the context of the Scriptures and their meaning. If time permits, consult other commentaries to expand your knowledge. Once you feel comfortable with the Scriptures, begin to plan the session by following these steps:

1. Read the session plan from GOD'S GIFT OF LOVE.
2. Refer to the session plan where you will find suggested activities that will help the participants engage the Scripture and activities to open the session and to close the session. Be aware that the activities generally include discussion; but some include art, music, movement, or other means of learning in addition to discussion.
3. When activities refer directly to GOD'S GIFT OF LOVE, mark the places in your book for easy reference during the session.
4. Gather supplies needed for each activity.
5. Select any hymn(s) you wish to use. If you will sing the hymn(s), notify your accompanist.
6. Determine how you will use the lectionary psalm or other additional reading.
7. Contact any guest speakers or assistants early in the week if you will use their services.

Helpful Ideas for Leading a Group

Bible studies come in many shapes, sizes, and formats. Some begin with a theme and find biblical support for it. Others begin with the Bible itself and unpack the Scriptures, whether from one book or several. Our study begins with the Bible, specifically the texts of the Revised Common Lectionary. Those Scriptures will deeply inform our study. However, GOD'S GIFT OF LOVE is not a "verse by verse" study of the readings. Instead, we are studying the texts as a kind of roadmap to guide us in our spiritual journey through the Advent season. Consequently, some of the suggested activities call participants to struggle with questions of faith in their own lives. Our focus is primarily on transformation so that participants may grow in their relationship with Jesus Christ and become more closely conformed to his image. That's a tall order for a five-week course! And it may be somewhat challenging for the participants since it may be far easier to discuss historical information about the Bible and consider various interpretations of a passage than it is to wrestle with what the passage says to them—personally and as a member of the body of Christ—in contemporary life.

Your role as the leader of this group is to create an environment in which participants will feel safe in raising their questions and expressing their doubts. You can also help the group feel comfortable by making clear that you rely solely on volunteers to answer questions and to read aloud. If adults feel pressed to respond or read, they may feel embarrassed and may not return to the group. If questions arise that you can definitely answer, do so. If you do not know the answer but suspect that an answer is available, say you do not know and offer to look it up and report back at the next session. Or, suggest a type of resource that will likely include the answer and challenge the questioner and others do some research and report back. Some questions cannot be fully answered, at least not in this life. Do not be afraid to point out that people through the ages have wrestled with some questions and yet they remain mysteries. If you can truly say so, respond that you have wrestled with that same question and have found an answer that works for you, or that you are still searching. When you show yourself to be a co-learner, the participants will feel more comfortable than if you act like the all-knowing expert. You will feel more at ease about leading the group as well.

Additional Scriptures for Advent

The additional Scriptures for this season come from the Psalms and Luke. Suggestions are given in some of the sessions for using these Scriptures, but you may want to try other options. For example, consider reading each psalm responsively, possibly adding the sung response if you are using the Psalter in your hymnal. Notice that the additional Scripture for the third Sunday of Advent is Luke 1:47-55, which is Mary's song of praise, also known as the "Magnificat." Some hymnals, such as *The United Methodist Hymnal*, include responsive readings with sung responses for Mary's "Magnificat" (199).

First Sunday in Advent: Psalm 122
Second Sunday in Advent: Psalm 72:1-7, 18-19
Third Sunday in Advent: Luke 1:47-55
Fourth Sunday in Advent: Psalm 80:1-7, 17-19
Christmas Eve: Psalm 96

GOD'S GIFT OF LOVE

1. Move Beyond the Time Famine

BIBLE BACKGROUND

During Advent, we look back in time to the incarnation of Jesus, who is God's gift of love with us; and we also look forward to the fulfillment of God's reign at the end of time. The readings for this first week of the season focus on the mystery and anticipation of God's reign. Although we will again celebrate Jesus' birth at Christmas, we recall that his coming as an infant is now viewed through the lens of his resurrection and his eagerly awaited coming again in glory. As those who live in the space between these two momentous events, we need to prepare ourselves and be alert for the consummation of the new age that dawned at his birth.

Isaiah 2:1-5

These prophetic words announce God's salvation. They are not addressed to any particular person, nor is the speaker identified, nor is there any clue as to when these words were written or when they will come to pass. This prophecy is also found in nearly identical form in Micah 4:1-3. Whether Micah's prophecy or Isaiah's came first is unknown. Some scholars believe that both prophets adopted this message from an even older tradition. Whatever was the case, this much is clear: This promise of salvation is meant to be heard by all the people in all nations. It is a universal offer open to all who will receive it.

Isaiah painted a glorious picture of the exalted Jerusalem, also known as Zion, as it will appear at the end of time. This "highest of the mountains" (verse 2)—the place where heaven and earth connect—will be the meeting place of God and all humanity. People will be making a pilgrimage to Zion so that God may instruct them, thereby enabling them to "walk in God's paths" (verse 3).

God is shown in a variety of roles in these verses. God is a teacher (verse 3) and a judge and arbiter who will "settle disputes" among the nations (verse 4). In response to God's actions, the people will transform their weapons of war into implements of agriculture. War will become a thing of the past. Peace will prevail. This familiar idea will ring again in the words of the host of angels who will praise God and declare peace on earth "among those whom [God] favors" on the night of Jesus' birth (Luke 2:14).

Verse 5 refers to the "house of Jacob," the Northern Kingdom of Israel. The "house of Jacob" stands in contrast to the *nations*, a word that includes non-Jews. Eventually, all nations—all people—will one day walk in the light of the Lord. For now, God's people are called to lead the way.*

Romans 13:11-14

Two Greek words carry different understandings of time: *Chronos* is time as measured by our clocks and calendars, and *kairos* is time measured by ripeness or readiness. We can check our watches to be ready for dinner at six o'clock, but we cannot predict when the tomatoes in our garden will be ready to serve for dinner. It carries the sense of expectation for what the appointed time will bring.

Although Paul was talking about waking up from sleep in verse 11, which to us would be time in the sense of *chronos*, the Greek word in this verse is *kairos*. Paul is referring to God's time when judgment and salvation will come. The time between today and the day of salvation is growing short. To prepare for the day of the dawning of the reign of God, Paul urged his readers to act "as people who live in the day" (verse 13). Darkness will give way to the light of God. People must choose whether they will live a lifestyle rooted in the world and its deeds of drunkenness, sexual immorality, arguing, and jealousy or a lifestyle rooted in a relationship with Christ. In verse 14, Paul wrote that believers are to "dress [themselves] with the Lord Jesus Christ" or "put on the Lord Jesus Christ" (NRSV) so that they may live according to the way of Christ. Although believers must make individual choices, the Greek word *you* in this passage is in the plural. Thus, Paul was not just calling individuals to a Christ-like lifestyle but rather was referring to entire church. Moral behavior was not simply a private concern but a corporate one.

During Advent, these verses help us to develop a sense of God's time. A new day dawned as the incarnate Lord walked upon the earth, but the time for the fulfillment of that reign when Christ comes again is yet to be revealed. As believers, we need to live expecting the reign of God to break in upon us and be constantly prepared for its coming.*

Matthew 24:36-44

In Matthew 24:1–25:46, we hear Jesus announce signs of his return, tell his disciples what life will be like in the meantime, and counsel them to live faithfully until he comes again. Today's passage from Matthew 24:36-44 focuses on the importance of being alert and prepared for his coming.

Despite the attempts of some Christians to pinpoint the exact time of his return, Jesus made clear that no one except God knows when that transforming event will occur. God's future action is revealed here, but God's timing remains a mystery known only to God. Since the timing is unknown, Jesus' followers must keep awake and alert. To underscore his point, Jesus used several examples. First, in verses 37-39, he reminded his listeners of the story of Noah. People were going about their normal routines, unaware of the coming catastrophe, when Noah entered the ark and God rained down a flood that "swept them all away" (verse 39). Notice that Jesus did not mention the people's wickedness that drove God to send a flood. Rather, his focus was on their unpreparedness for this act of judgment. Jesus pointed out that the day of the Lord will be just like that. He went on in verses 40 and 41 to give examples of men and women minding their daily business when some would be taken and others would be left at their work posts. In one final example, Jesus pointed out that if a homeowner knew a thief was coming, he would have been vigilant and not allowed his home to be burglarized (verse 43).

As we begin this Advent season with our thoughts of a baby soon to born, Jesus' images of a disastrous flood, people being taken, and a robber may jar us. These are disturbing images. But they also serve Jesus' point: Things happen when we least expect them. For that reason, we must be ever watchful, alert, and prepared for his return.*

SESSION PLAN

Open the Session

Create a personal time chart.

Distribute paper and pencils or markers. Ask participants to draw a large circle on the paper and then draw lines to divide the circle into twenty-four "slices." Each "slice" represents one hour. Participants are to label each "slice" with activities they are engaged in on a day of their choice during the month of December. For example, a participant who sleeps seven hours per night would label seven "slices" as "sleep." Perhaps another two "slices" would be labeled "meals." Possibly eight "slices" would be labeled "work."

After providing time for participants to finish, ask: Would you say that during this Advent season you have a time feast—that is, plenty of time to do what you want and need to do—or a time famine? If participants have been able to read the study guide prior to the session, ask: How might the ideas you read about in this week's lesson help you to rearrange your time to help you better prepare to welcome Christ?

Offer an opening prayer

Gracious God, you have given us a priceless gift of love in sending your Beloved Son to us. Empower us to use our time wisely as we prepare to celebrate his coming in the flesh and his coming again in glory. In Jesus' name we pray, Amen.

Engage the Scriptures

Reflect on a peaceful new beginning in Isaiah 2:1-5.

Ask a volunteer to read Isaiah 2:1-5. Share information from the Bible Background. Review highlights of the section "About Those Plows" in the study book.

Distribute paper and pencils. Invite participants to listen as you read Isaiah 2:1-5 again. This time they are either to write on the paper or underline in their Bibles two words or phrases that captured their attention.

Have participants form teams of two or three. Ask the teams to discuss the following questions:

1. What words or phrases did you select?
2. Why do these words seem important?
3. How might these words guide you during your journey through Advent?

Suggest that participants allow these words to continue "marinating" in the week ahead to see what new insights come to mind.

Respond to a sculpture of peace.

Download and print a picture of the bronze sculpture "Let Us Beat Our Swords into Ploughshares" prior to the session. The government of the Soviet Union presented this sculpture, which was created by Soviet artist Evgeny Vuchetich, to the United Nations on December 4, 1959. It is located in the North Garden of the United Nations Headquarters.

Show this picture and ask: How does this sculpture, based on words from Isaiah 2:4, help you envision the reign of God and give you hope for the future?

Set a spiritual alarm clock according to Romans 13:11-14.

Have a kitchen timer on hand. Prior to the session, enlist a participant to secretly set the time for three minutes and place it out of sight so it will count down during this activity. Ask the following questions :
1. How do you feel about being awakened in the morning?
2. Are you ready for the day and anxious to fulfill whatever plans you have, or would you prefer to pull the covers up and stay and bed?
3. Why do you feel the way you do?

Hopefully, the alarm will go off during this discussion. Encourage participants to note one another's reactions. Then, direct participants to read Romans 13:11-14 silently.

Review highlights of "A Spiritual Alarm Clock" and read aloud the final two paragraphs of this section. Use this novel situation to help participants think about the kinds of wake-up experiences they have had, for example, a job change, a health crisis, or change in family status. Ask:
1. How have these wake-up calls affected your spiritual life?
2. In what ways have they made you more aware of the presence of the incarnate Christ in your life?
3. What changes did you make as a result of a wake-up call?

Describe the "end times."

Post a large sheet of paper and encourage participants to write words or phrases to describe the "end times" when Christ will come again. You may also invite participants to make sketches of their ideas about the end times.

Ask: How does focusing on the end of time empower you to live in the present? How does that focus prompt you to live faithfully as Jesus' disciple?

Discover the message of Matthew 24:36-44.

Read Matthew 24:36-44. Ask: Without opening your Bible to review, what did you hear as the take-home message of this passage? (Hear responses and then summarize the message in words such as: "The Son of Man will return in glory at the end of time but we cannot know when that will be and, therefore, must keep alert at all times.") Ask: How do the four examples in verses 37-39, 40, 41, and 43 reinforce Matthew's message? (In each case, there is a sudden unexpected change that comes in the midst of one's daily life. Add information from Bible Background as appropriate.)

Review highlights of "Nobody Knows the Day or the Hour." What steps can you take to help you stay alert and be prepared? What difference would taking these steps make in the quality of your life?

Prepare for the coming of Christ.

Recall that all of today's Scripture readings have pointed us toward a future time when Christ will return and the just, peaceable kingdom of God will be fully revealed. For now, we are living in the time between the incarnation of Jesus as a baby and his coming again in glory as King of kings and Lord of lords. We do not know when Christ will return, so as we live in this in-between time, we must keep alert.

Ask: How will you keep alert so you will be prepared for Christ's coming? List these ideas on a large sheet of paper. Here are some suggestions: Set aside time daily to read and reflect on a passage of Scripture; use a "breath prayer" such as "Jesus, Savior, calm my spirit" whenever you feel stressed or pressed for time; give the gift of your time to someone who needs you; meditate on your relationship with Jesus.

Encourage participants to each select at least one of these ideas that will help them stay focused on the importance of spiritual readiness during the fleeting time of this Advent season. Distribute paper and pencils so participants may record their choices. Suggest that they refer to these papers throughout the season so that they can recall their choices and hold themselves accountable for making appropriate preparations.

Close the Session

Read Psalm 122 as words of blessing.

Distribute hymnals that include a Psalter or have participants turn to Psalm 122 in their Bibles. Read this psalm responsively as noted in the Psalter or by alternating odd and even verses in the Bible.

Ask each participant to face a partner and repeat these words adapted from verses 8 and 9: Peace be with you, [name]. . . . I will pray for your good.

Offer a closing prayer.

Giver of every good and perfect gift, we pray for the gift of your peace in the midst of our hectic lives. Heal those places wounded by trying to keep the frantic pace of the world. Open our hearts to the mysteries of your coming and coming again so that we may spend our time preparing to receive you. Amen.

2. Preconception, Reconception, and Conception

BIBLE BACKGROUND

The reign of God is coming! That reign, which will be ushered in by a king from the stump of David's line, will be one of righteousness and justice. Knowing that God has promised such a king brings hope to all, but especially to those on the margins of society. John the Baptist came out of the wilderness, appearing much as the great prophet Elijah had centuries before him, to issue a call to repentance. The kingdom of God was drawing very near. People had to prepare their hearts and be baptized for the forgiveness of their sins in order to be ready to receive God's gift of love.

Isaiah 11:1-10

This oracle concerning the ideal king is closely related to Isaiah 9:1-7, which is the reading for Christmas Eve. Both oracles may have been included in King Hezekiah's coronation ceremony. Jesse (verse 1) was David's father; thus, a shoot emerging from the stump of Jesse refers to a new king in the Davidic line. The branch image (verse 1), which symbolizes an ideal king, is also found in the books of Jeremiah and Zechariah. The spirit of the Lord will equip this king with wisdom, understanding, planning, strength, and knowledge (verse 2). The righteousness of this king will be evident in the way he cares for the poor and other vulnerable people who live on society's fringes (verse 4).

The leadership of this new king will have far-reaching consequences, affecting even nature. No longer will the prey—the lamb, the goat, the calf, and the cow—need to fear its predator—the wolf, the leopard, the lion, and the bear, respectively. The creatures of God's creation will live in such harmony that their offspring will even sleep next to one another. The fierce lion will no longer hunt for meat, but will instead eat straw. Not only will the relationship between creatures within the animal kingdom be changed but so too will the relationship between the animal kingdom and humanity. Young children will be able to play without fear near holes of poisonous snakes and not be harmed.

This peaceable world, which will be inaugurated when Israel and Judah are restored, will be marked by "the knowledge of the LORD" (verse 9). Such knowledge will not be limited, but rather will cover the earth "just as the water covers the sea" (verse 9). The center of this tranquil world will be God's "holy mountain" (verse 9), which is the Temple Mount in Jerusalem.

Although this prophetic passage is not cited in the New Testament, it is read during Advent because early Christian tradition traced Isaiah's vision of an ideal king from David's line to its fulfillment in Jesus.*

Romans 15:4-13

This passage begins and ends with the theme of hope. In verse 4, Paul advised his readers to find that hope within the Scriptures. Paul concluded this section with a benediction in verse 13 asking "the God of hope" to fill believers so that they may "overflow with hope." Paul was not equating hope to wishful thinking, as we might when we say things like, "I hope I get a new car for Christmas." Instead, because Paul believed that God was the source of our hope, he affirmed that we can trust and believe that whatever God promises will come to pass.

A second important theme in this passage is harmony. Earlier in Romans, Paul had explained that the promises God made to Israel long ago have been fulfilled in Jesus. Moreover, God's intention was to include not only Jews but also Gentiles in the community of faith. That coming together was happening, but it was not always smooth. The gospel was for both Jews and Gentiles, but they had lived very differently; now they were being challenged to find unity in Christ Jesus. Verse 7 summarizes this need to join with one another: "So welcome each another, in the same way that Christ also welcomed you, for God's glory." The Greek word translated here as "welcome" does not simply refer to shaking hands or offering a cup of coffee. Jews and Gentiles are to offer mutual hospitality so that God's circle of love is expanded to include all. Boundaries between insiders and outsiders have been erased, since God has already welcomed everyone (see Galatians 3:28). Therefore, believers are to welcome others just as God has already done.

Paul included several quotations from the Scriptures in verses 9-12 to show that the inclusion of the Gentiles was not an afterthought, but rather was part of God's plan of salvation from the beginning. Verse 9 quotes Psalm 18:49 and 2 Samuel 22:50; verse 10, Deuteronomy 32:43; verse 11, Psalm 117:1; and verse 12, Isaiah 11:10. *

Matthew 3:1-12

John the Baptist is associated with Jesus' baptism when Jesus was about thirty years old. John challenged his listeners to prepare for the One who was coming to judge and baptize with fire. Reliance on one's ancestral tree, even if it can be traced to Abraham, is not enough. Each person must have a changed heart.

John stood in the gap between the end of the Old Testament era and the beginning of the New. According the Matthew 3:3, he fulfilled the words of the prophet Isaiah (40:3), though there is some variation in the wording as to where the voice is located. Moreover, John appeared out of the wilderness as the prophet Elijah had (verse 4; compare 2 Kings 1:8). Both men lived austerely. John's connection with Elijah is critically important, for Malachi had prophesied that Elijah would come back to prepare people for the coming of the day of the Lord (3:1; 4:5). As we will explore further in our next session, Jesus referred to John as the fulfillment of Malachi 3:1 (Matthew 11:10) and also said he was Elijah (Matthew 11:14).

Although Matthew 3:1 reports that John was in the desert, his message of repentance was reaching "people from Jerusalem, throughout Judea, and all around the Jordan River" (verse 5). John called them to change their ways and turn toward God. Usually the Temple in Jerusalem was the place where people went to confess their sins and, through the priests, offer sacrifices for their sins. Here, though, this prophet on the margins was functioning as one who was associated with the Temple cult. No wonder the religious establishment had come to see what was happening. John referred to them as "children of snakes" (verse 7), which we can almost envision slithering away from the fires of judgment that cannot be extinguished.

In contrast to those images of judgment, John also used images of hope. He spoke about his baptism with water and the Coming One's baptism "with the Holy Spirit and with fire" (verse 11).*

SESSION PLAN

Open the Session

Make a Jesse Tree.

Gather supplies prior to the session to create a Jesse tree. You will need a dead branch, a pot, and some stones or dirt to hold the branch upright in the pot. (If these supplies are not available, use craft paper to draw a tree limb.) Have construction paper, scissors, markers, and yarn or string on hand.

Post a list of possible symbols that participants can make for the tree such as creation, snake, rainbow, tent of Abraham, Jacob's ladder, Joseph's coat, Ten Commandments, King David's crown, Bible, star, manger, and so on.

Explain that the purpose of the Jesse Tree is to tell the story of God's plan of salvation by using symbols, one for each day of Advent, beginning with creation and ending on Christmas with a symbol for the birth of Jesus. Note that the idea for this tree, which has been used since the Middle Ages, comes from today's reading from Isaiah 11, which refers to "the stump of Jesse" (verse 1). We are going to reconceive this dead limb by making it into a "living" branch that holds reminders of God's faithfulness and redemption.

Hang some of the symbols participants create, such as the creation and snake, on the tree this week. Add others in subsequent weeks.

Suggest that participants make a tree for their own homes. Books with symbols (or symbol patterns) and family devotions are available.

Offer an opening prayer.

God of our Fathers and Mothers, help us to see the great story of your salvation as told throughout the Scriptures. As we place symbols on our Jesse tree, we give thanks that we are part of this ongoing story of your love. Amen.

Engage the Scriptures

Discover the prophecy of Isaiah 11:1-10.

Introduce today's reading and its primary image ("the stump of Jesse") by selecting someone to read the first two paragraphs of "Put a Brick on It." Ask: Where have you seen new life come out of old?

Choose two volunteers, one to read Isaiah 11:1-5 and the other to read verses 6-10.

Discuss these questions, adding information from the Old Testament Bible Background:

1. What are the traits of the new shoot that will grow from Jesse's stump?
2. What kinds of actions does the prophet expect this person to take?
3. How will all creation be different because this new branch has sprouted from Jesse's stump?
4. Why, do you think, did the early church see Jesus as the fulfillment of this prophecy?

Read a psalm about God's reign.

Note that today's lectionary psalm is 72:1-7, 18-19. Invite participants to turn to this psalm in their Bibles and ask half of the group read verses 1-7 and the other half read verses 18-19. As an option, distribute hymnals and read whatever part of Psalm 72 is found in the Psalter. Use a sung response for Advent.

Ask: What similarities do you see between the king portrayed here and the one in Isaiah 11? Do you see Jesus here, as the early church recognized him in Isaiah 11? Why or why not?

Ponder Paul's Teaching in Romans 15:4-13.

Read aloud Romans 15:4-13 as participants follow along in their Bibles. Ask these questions. Add information from the Epistle Bible Background as appropriate.
1. What does this passage say about the Scriptures of the past? (verses 4-6).
2. Jews and Gentiles both belong to the church in Rome. What does Paul say about each welcoming the other? (verses 7-9)
3. What point was Paul making by quoting Old Testament Scriptures in verses 9-12? (Refer to the third paragraph of "When Stumped.")
4. What themes does Paul seem to highlight?
5. How do you see these themes of hope and harmony being lived out in today's church?
6. How might Paul's teaching help the church to reconceive these themes of hope and harmony?

Learn about John the Baptist in Matthew 3:1-6.

Select a volunteer to read Matthew 3:1-6 while participants envision John the Baptist. Ask:
1. How would you describe John's physical appearance?
2. Would his appearance cause you to link him with any other biblical figure? If so, who? (See the second paragraph of the Gospel Bible Background.)

3. Is there an actor who comes to mind when you imagine John speaking?
4. Had you been among the throngs of people coming to meet John, what would your first impression of him have been?
5. Would John have met your expectations as the "voice" that Isaiah prophesied would shout out? Why or why not?

Respond to John the Baptist's message in Matthew 3:7-12.

Suggest that participants silently review "Fear, Water, and Fire" to prepare themselves for John's message.

Choose someone to read John's words in Matthew 3:7b-12. Begin this section by reading 7a yourself.

Distribute paper and pencils. Invite participants to reflect on the following questions that you will read aloud. Pause after each one to allow time for those who wish to do so to write their answers. Before you begin, state that these responses are confidential.
1. What do you need to repent of right now?
2. How has baptism changed your life? Or, if you have not been baptized, what barriers do you need to overcome to receive this sacrament?
3. What fruits have you produced that show that your heart and life have changed?

Conclude by suggesting that participants review their responses and be open to making changes as God leads them.

Visualize God's coming reign of justice and peace.

Prior to the session, locate a copy of one of the paintings in the nineteenth century Quaker artist Edward Hicks's series "Peaceable Kingdom." These pictures are easily found online, in books, and often in churches.

Observe that all of today's Scriptures have helped us to look ahead to the coming reign of God. This reign will reconceptualize our usual understanding of how people live together since it will be marked by peace, harmony, hope, and justice.

Show the picture either by holding it up or passing it around if the copy is small. Allow time for participants to think about how this picture captures their own hopes for the coming Kingdom.

Invite participants to call out words or phrases that have come to mind.

Close the Session

Offer prayers for those who need to hear good news.

Read: Recall the messages of hope we have heard today. God's kingdom is coming! The prophet described it; Paul explained its meaning; and John the Baptist preached repentance so that all might be ready to enter into this new Kingdom. Think of at least one person you know who needs to hear this message of hope. Pray silently for that person, asking God to give you opportunities this week to share this message in such a powerful way that your friend, family member, or coworker will risk a new beginning by choosing life in Jesus Christ.

Conclude the silent prayer time by praying aloud: Gracious God of peace and hope, open our hearts and minds to the new life that you have for us. Empower us to be ready to welcome Jesus, who brings this new life, by repenting of our sins and turning to you. In the name of the Coming One we pray, Amen.

3. Sacrament: Finding the Holy in the Ordinary

BIBLE BACKGROUND

God's gift of love will soon be here. We can catch glimpses of this new day as we discover the transformation of the land and its people that Isaiah made known to us—an arid desert that has come alive with abundant vegetation. On that day of salvation, the blind, deaf, lame, and mute will be healed. At his coming in the flesh, Jesus will heal and preach good news to the poor. As we begin this third week of Advent, we are anxious to welcome a baby, but James counseled us to be patient as we wait for the coming of the Lord.

Isaiah 35:1-10

In this joyous oracle, God promised to redeem those held captive in Babylon and bring them home to Zion. This journey will in some ways be like a second Exodus, though in other ways it will be quite different. The first Exodus of the newly liberated Hebrew slaves from Egypt entailed an arduous forty-year journey through a barren wilderness. God was clearly present with the people, but they endured tests and hardship. In contrast, this second journey will be through a transformed landscape—a blossoming desert where water is abundant and singing is heard. The trek along "The Holy Way" (verse 8) will be safe. Neither animal predators nor people who are not among the "redeemed" (verse 9) will be on the road. The path of this road will be clearly marked so no one will get lost.

This text describes great reversals: People will be healed of their infirmities, the fearful ones will find courage, and the arid landscape will be changed so that nature itself will teem with life in the wilderness. The highway upon which the people walk will take them from a land of punishment and despair to a future filled with hope.

These words from Isaiah mesh well with the hopeful message of Advent. God can and does transform our world. God's gift of love and salvation is coming. As scholar Bruce Birch has written, "God's coming signals a future for those who have given in to hopelessness and sorrow. In God, wilderness becomes not a journey of struggle but of hope, and the Advent season rekindles this hope for a way through the wilderness anew each year."[1]

The response to God's salvation is joyous praise. The third Sunday of Advent is sometimes referred to as *Gaudete,* a Latin word which means "rejoice." Just as God's people rejoiced along the way home, so we who are now on the Advent journey also rejoice as we draw closer to the celebration of the arrival God's Messiah.*

James 5:7-10

Thought to have been written by James, the brother of Jesus, who was the head of the church in Jerusalem from about A.D. 36 until his martyrdom in A.D. 62, this letter was addressed to "the twelve tribes who are scattered outside the land of Israel" (1:1). In his letter, James addressed ethical and moral issues, with a particular emphasis on the treatment of the poor and speaking with care so as not to harm others.

In this final chapter, James called Christians to "be patient as you wait for the coming of the Lord" (verse 7). James often used illustrations to make his point, as we see here at the end of verse 7. Early rain was needed to soften the ground to receive seed; late rain had to fall to allow the grain to ripen. The Palestinian farmer certainly could not control the rain, nor did he have access to irrigated water. Consequently, the farmer must wait patiently, believing that God in faithfulness to the covenant will provide the needed water (see Deuteronomy 11:14; Jeremiah 5:24; Hosea 6:3). Similarly, those who wait for "the coming of the Lord" (verse 8), the return of Christ, must wait patiently and behave appropriately. That day will bring both judgment and salvation.

In verse 9, James warned his readers not to complain about one another. Here he referred not to outsiders but rather to church insiders. Those who grumble and judge others will themselves be judged, just as Jesus had said (Matthew 7:1). James' comment that "the judge is standing at the door" echoed Jesus' words in Matthew 24:33; Mark 13:29; and Luke 12:36.

James used the prophets as examples of people who patiently endured suffering (verse 10). The theme of the suffering prophet is found in other Christian Scriptures such as Matthew 5:12; 23:29-39. James' point here is that servants of God will not escape harassment and persecution. The opposite is true: Christians suffer because they are faithful to God. *

Matthew 11:2-11

This week's Gospel lesson continues to focus on John the Baptist. Recall from last week that John stood in the gap between the end of the former age and the beginning of the new age being revealed in Jesus. In Matthew 3, we heard John preaching and calling people to repentance in order to be prepared to receive the Messiah.

The scene in Matthew 11 is radically different. John was no longer preaching but had been arrested (4:12). (Matthew 14:1-12 explains the reason for John's imprisonment and the events that led to his death.) While in jail, John had heard more about Jesus, so he dispatched several of his disciples to inquire as to whether Jesus was or was not the long-awaited One. Jesus relied on his actions to disclose his identity. These actions—healing the blind and lame and deaf, cleansing those with skin diseases, raising the dead, and preaching good news to the poor—were the same actions that Isaiah envisioned as part of God's coming reign of righteousness and justice. In verse 6, Jesus blessed those who recognized his identity.

In verses 7-11, Jesus spoke with the crowds about John the Baptist. Clearly, John was not part of any elite cultic leadership. Instead, he lived an austere life in the wilderness, which is where the people to whom Jesus was speaking had gone to see John. Jesus affirmed that John was indeed a prophet, but much more than that. Verse 10 makes the link again between John and the prophecy in Malachi 3:1 concerning a messenger to be sent by God to prepare the way of the Lord. Jesus proclaimed that no one had been born who was greater than John. Yet, the least in the Kingdom was greater than John (verse 11).

Notice in verse 14, which is beyond today's reading, that Jesus identified John as Elijah, the prophet who was expected to return "before the great and terrifying day of the LORD arrives" (Malachi 4:5).*

SESSION PLAN

Open the Session

Observe how one person finds the holy in the ordinary.

Read: Brother Lawrence was an uneducated, lay Carmelite brother who worked in a monastery kitchen during the seventeenth century. His insights into life with God were recorded in a book titled *The Practice of the Presence of God: The Best Rule of Holy Life.* He was known for his ability to be constantly aware of and in communion with God. At the end of his "Fourth Conversation," we read: "The time of business does not with me differ from the time of prayer; and in the noise and clutter of my kitchen, while several persons are at the same time calling for different things, I possess GOD in as great tranquility as if I were upon my knees at the Blessed Sacrament."[2]

Invite participants to ponder this question and respond: How are you, like Brother Lawrence, able to find the holy in the ordinary routines of life?

Offer an opening prayer.

Gracious God, help us to encounter you not only in the sanctuary but also in our homes and all the places in which we find ourselves each day. Tune us in so that we may experience your presence every moment of our lives. In Jesus' name we pray, Amen.

Engage the Scriptures

Enact a return through fertile wilderness.

Invite participants to read Isaiah 35:1-10 silently. Remind them that these words were first heard by exiled Israelites in Babylon, who would have been very excited to hear this prophesy about their return home. As participants read, they are to think about any motions or movements that could illustrate this passage, such as smiling, raising hands in the air, opening their eyes wide, jumping, or walking purposefully.

Encourage those who are able to stand and walk with you around the learning area as you read, making appropriate motions as they go. (Suggest that those who choose not to walk make simple motions while seated.) Start by reading verses 1-2. As these verses are read, participants are to make simple motions to illustrate what you have read. Lead the group to a different space in the room to read verses 3-7. Again, participants may make any motions that seem to them to illustrate the images. Continue the journey together to a third space and read verses 8-10. Participants will make motions. Point out that in the act of walking they have embodied the message of journeying.

When all are seated, ask: If you can imagine returning home with the exiles through a wilderness that has become well-watered and fertile, what can you imagine about something in your own life or church that seems dead springing to life again?

Relate James's teaching on patience to our lives.

Set the stage by asking a volunteer to read the first paragraph of "Patience, Patience." Call on a volunteer to read James 5:7-10.

Invite participants to remember instances in their own lives as children or teenagers when their patience was stretched to the limit, perhaps waiting for a special event. Ask:

1. How might patience help you to live more sacramentally, that is, by being aware of God's presence in your daily life?
2. James linked patience and suffering of the prophets in 5:10 (NRSV). What examples can you give to illustrate how you or those you know have been patient in suffering?
3. What steps might you take to exercise greater patience?
4. James observed that we need patience as we await the coming of the Lord. What challenges do you face in awaiting Christ's return?

Explore Mary's Song of Praise.

Select a volunteer to read Luke 1:47-55. Or, if you have access to a hymnal with "Canticle of Mary" (see page 199 of *The United Methodist Hymnal*), read this song responsively.

Discuss these questions:

1. What do you learn from this song, known as the "Magnificat," about Mary's relationship with God?
2. What do you learn about God?
3. What do you learn about how the world will be changed?
4. What do you learn about God's relationship with Israel?

Discern Jesus' identity.

Choose a volunteer to read Matthew 11:2-6. Review highlights of "Are You the One?"

Discuss these questions. Use information from "Are You the One?" and the Bible Background to broaden the discussion.

1. Given what we read about John last week in Matthew 3, what do you make of him sending messengers to inquire about Jesus' identity?
2. How did Jesus answer John's question? (Note that he did not give John a yes or no answer. Instead, he pointed to his actions to summarize his mission.)
3. What connection do you see among these actions? (They describe life in God's kingdom, as prophesied by Isaiah in 26:19; 29:18-19; 35:5-6; 42:7; 61:1. Ask participants to turn to these verses.)
4. What does Jesus' response to John suggest to you about living day by day as a follower of Christ? How can you be the hands and feet of the Messiah?

Hear Jesus praise John.

Recommend that participants silently review "Are You the One?"
Choose someone to read Matthew 11:7-11 and ask:

1. How did Jesus describe John? (Note these words that point to different aspects of John. The "reed" (NRSV) or "stalk" (CEB) refers to a known symbol for Herod, whom John challenged. That image could also describe a holy man who is as thin as a reed. The one in refined clothes refers to a king. Jesus also said John was a prophet but more than a prophet. In verse 14, he referred to him as Elijah.)*
2. What do Jesus' words about the ministry of John as "preparing the way" for God's kingdom through Jesus Christ suggest to you about your role in God's kingdom? How can your life become a sacrament demonstrating the presence of Christ?

Close the Session

Follow the example of Brother Lawrence.

Recall that we began our session with words from Brother Lawrence. Read these words about him: "So, likewise, in his business in the kitchen (to which he had naturally a great aversion), having accustomed himself to do everything there for the love of GOD, and with prayer, upon all occasions, for His grace to do his work well, he had found everything easy, during the fifteen years that he had been employed there."[3]

Distribute paper and pencils. Invite participants to think of work that they do not like to do. Suggest that they prayerfully write a commitment to

GOD'S GIFT OF LOVE

God to pray for grace to do this work well. Encourage them to take note of how spending time with God in the midst of a chore makes the work easier and enriches their relationship with God.

Offer a closing prayer.

God who is lovingly present in all the days and ways of our lives, we ask that by your grace we may draw closer to your holiness amid the mundane tasks of our daily lives. In Jesus' name we pray, Amen.

4. Scavenging for Advent

BIBLE BACKGROUND

We have reached the point this fourth week in our Advent journey where a betrothed young woman is now carrying a son, and her husband-to-be learns in a dream that her child is of the Holy Spirit. Joseph accepted Mary as his wife and her child as his adopted son. The angel proclaimed that he was to be named Jesus (Emmanuel), just as the prophet Isaiah had foretold. Paul reminded us that the coming of God's Son had been promised many years ago and announced by the prophets. The child's long-anticipated arrival was set within the context of God's gracious activity in human history.

Isaiah 7:10-16

This passage is part of the story of the encounter between Isaiah and King Ahaz, a descendant of King David who ruled Judah from 735–715 B.C. Isaiah 7:1 refers to King Rezin of Aram (Syria) and King Pekah of Israel (also known as Ephraim or the Northern Kingdom). Rezin and Pekah formed a coalition to stand against the powerful Assyrians ruled by Tiglath-pileser III. Ahaz refused to join this coalition, but he was so terrified of these two enemies that he wanted to become an ally of their Assyrian enemies. During a conflict known as the Syro-Ephraimite war (735–732 B.C.), Rezin and Pekah attacked Ahaz in order to coerce him to unite with them. The story is told in such a way that the reader knows from verse 1 that the attack was unsuccessful, thereby showing that God could and would protect Judah and the Davidic monarchy.

In verses 10-11, God encouraged Ahaz to ask for a sign concerning what he should do; but Ahaz refused, claiming he would not put God to the test. Actually, Ahaz did not want a sign that would discourage him from entering into an alliance with Assyria. Judah need not enter into an alliance with foreign powers, for God would protect them; but the king clearly did not trust God for such protection. Isaiah told Ahaz that God would give him a sign anyway. That sign was a pregnant woman whose child was to be named Immanuel (verse 14). Verses 15-16 point out the transitory nature of this military threat from Rezin and Pekah: Very soon—before this child was old enough to make choices—the threat will have ended. Judah will be so safe that special foods such as "butter and honey" can be imported to Jerusalem.

This sign of a child is also the sign that Christians eagerly await during Advent. Although Isaiah 8:3 identified Isaiah's wife ("the prophetess") as the mother of this yet-to-be-born child, Christians understand the young, pregnant woman of prophecy to be Mary.*

Romans 1:1-7

In the ancient Greek and Roman world, a letter generally began with the name of the sender, the name of the addressee, and a short greeting. Paul's salutation followed that format, but it is expanded to include information about Paul and God's sending of Jesus.

In verse 1, Paul described himself as a "slave," an "apostle," and as one "set apart." These words reveal much about how Paul perceived himself in relation to Jesus. First, he was completely dedicated to him and willing to serve. Second, as an apostle, he was sent out to minister on behalf of Christ. Finally, he had been commissioned for the purpose of sharing the good news.

Verses 2-4 make clear that this good news was not an afterthought; rather, it fulfilled a promise God made long ago, had announced through the prophets, and was recorded in the Scriptures. The gospel concerns the person of Jesus Christ, a descendant of King David who "was publicly identified as God's Son with power through his resurrection from the dead, which was based on the Spirit of holiness" (verse 4).

Verses 5-6 spell out Paul's role: By God's grace, he was called to "bring all Gentiles to faithful obedience." Paul's readers in the Roman church, which he had neither founded nor visited, had become increasingly Gentile after A.D. 49 when the emperor Claudius decreed the expulsion of Jews from the city because they created disturbances. They began to return after Claudius' death in A.D. 54; so when Paul wrote this letter to the Roman Church in A.D. 57, the congregation included both Jews and Gentiles. This longest salutation of any of Paul's letters concludes in verse 7. Addressing both his Jewish and Gentile readers, "saints" means "to be set apart for the gospel of God" in both Hebrew and Greek.

As we read this passage on the fourth Sunday of Advent, we focus on the good news of Jesus Christ, which had been foretold by the prophets and proclaimed by Paul, and our response to the Son of God.*

Matthew 1:18-25

The genealogy in Matthew 1:1-16 connects Jesus with both David, Israel's great king to whom God promised an everlasting dynasty (2 Samuel 7:1-17), and Abraham, the patriarch with whom God made a covenant promise to bless "all the families of the earth" (Genesis 12:3). Verse 16 records that Mary's husband Joseph was descended from David's line. Yet there is a problem that verses 18-25 must resolve: Jesus was said to be the "son of David;" but Joseph, who is in David's line, was not Jesus' biological father. Thus, these verses must explain Jesus' origins.

The lengthy nativity story in Luke focuses on Mary, but in Matthew's telling all we know about Mary is that she and Joseph were betrothed and that she was pregnant. Betrothal, which normally ended with marriage when the bride was 12 or 13 years of age, was different from our concept of engagement. Whereas an engagement can be broken, an ancient betrothal was tantamount to marriage. Should either party die, the other would become a widow or widower. Likewise, unfaithfulness was considered adultery, which necessitated a divorce, even though the couple had not yet lived together or consummated the marriage.*

Whereas Luke's story spotlighted Mary's response to Gabriel, Matthew's story explored Joseph's response to the news of Mary's pregnancy. He was said to be a "righteous man" (verse 19) who had no interest in humiliating Mary by subjecting her to a public divorce. Having made the decision to quietly end their relationship, Joseph was visited by an angel in a dream. The angel explained to him that the child Mary was carrying was of divine origin. Her son, who was to be named Jesus (*Yeshua* in Hebrew), would fulfill the prophecy of Isaiah 7:14. Trusting God, Joseph wed the pregnant Mary rather than divorcing her, though they did not have marital relations until the child was born. Joseph's naming of the baby signified his adoption of this divine child into the line of David.*

SESSION PLAN

Open the Session

Go on a scavenger hunt.

Collect Christmas-themed items prior to the session. Arrive early and place them around the room. Some may be in plain sight; others may be somewhat hidden. Items could include greeting cards, ornaments, Christmas stockings, sheet music or compact discs of Christmas music, holiday napkins, Advent calendars, Jesse Trees, cookie cutters, Advent wreaths, candles, wrapping paper, and whatever else you have available.

Form teams of three or four, set a time limit, define parameters for the hunt (inside the room or whatever areas you choose), and ask the teams to find and collect Christmas-themed items.

Call time and bring everyone together. Have the teams count and report on the number of items they have found.

End this activity with quiet time by asking participants to focus on just one item that they have scavenged and ponder this question: How does this item help me to focus on the meaning of God's gift of love in Jesus?

Offer an opening prayer.

O Lord, as we gather during these closing days of Advent, may we set aside our weariness to come apart from the bustle of this season and listen for your voice, perhaps speaking through objects as simple as greeting cards. Show us your dream for our lives so we may faithfully do your will and serve others as you call us to do. In the name of Emmanuel we pray, Amen.

Engage the Scriptures

Explore the sign of Immanuel.

Review highlights of the Bible Background for Isaiah 7:10-16, then read the Scripture aloud. Review highlights of "World Weary." Discuss these questions:
1. Why did Ahaz refuse to seek a sign from God?
2. Isaiah wrote in verse 13 about wearying people and God. In what ways did Ahaz weary God?
3. Despite Ahaz's refusal, God gave a sign (verse 14). What was that sign? How might it be interpreted in Isaiah's day? in our day?
4. When have you been too weary to see signs of God's promise in your life?

5. If you are feeling weary right now, what can you do to resist this weariness in order to scavenge meaning in this Advent season?

Discuss meanings of "Set Apart."

Select a volunteer to read Romans 1:1-7.

Encourage participants to review the first two paragraphs of "Set Apart." Form several small teams. Post these questions on a large sheet of paper for each team to discuss. Suggest that they look at the Bible Background for Romans 1:1-7.

1. What did Paul reveal about himself in these verses?
2. For what purpose was he "set apart"?
3. How would you describe the difference between being "set aside" and "set apart"?
4. What actions do you think Paul would want your church to take on behalf of those who feel that they have been "set aside"?
5. How does the idea that you are "set apart" for service to God enhance your Advent journey?

Respond to a dream.

Read or review highlights of the Bible Background for Matthew 1:18-25 to inform participants about the marriage customs of first-century Palestine and read the Scripture aloud.

Invite participants to imagine themselves as Joseph and silently answer his questions as you read this script:

I thought Mary would make a wonderful wife. But now this! Who could have imagined she'd be unfaithful to me? I know the law says I'm to divorce her; but I just cannot disgrace her so publicly, even though she is pregnant and I'm sure the baby isn't mine. How can I be true to my own principles and protect Mary? I feel confused and tired. Perhaps a nap will help. (pause)

(Yawn.) I was dreaming. I know I was. But it all seemed so real. An angel came and told me to wed Mary anyway because her child was God's child. What a wild notion! What am I going to do? (pause)

Bring participants together and ask: What new insights did you gain concerning Joseph's character, his quandary, and his relationship with God?

Talk about "Listening to the Dream"

Read or review highlights of "Listening to the Dream." Form teams of two or three. Ask the teams to discuss the following questions: How do you respond to Joseph's willingness to listen to his dream? When have you enjoyed taking the backroads or the long way home? How does this image describe unconventional choices in your life? How might you "declutter" your life in order to scavenge for meaning by listening more carefully to God's dream for your life?

Appreciate the meaning of Advent.

Call on four volunteers to each read one paragraph of the introduction to "Scavenging for Advent."

Distribute paper and pencils. Invite participants to recall today's Bible readings, Chapter 4 in the study book, and ideas from the discussions. Then they are to list as many answers as possible for this question: What new meanings and insights have you scavenged from today's lesson that will enrich your appreciation of God's gift of love in Jesus? Go around the room and ask each participant for one response. As time permits, continue to go around the room, but limit each participant to one response per round.

Close the Session

Listen for God.

Read: Recall that God spoke through an angel in a dream to Joseph. The message that he heard radically changed his life. In what ways does God speak to you? Do you hear God's voice in the Scriptures, through a sermon, in the sacraments of baptism and Holy Communion, in a dream, through art or music, in Christmas-themed objects, during prayer and meditation, as you take a walk or hike? Be alert this week for the ways in which God speaks to you. Jot down these ways and the messages that God is giving you in a journal or on a sheet of paper. As soon as you feel ready, begin to act on what you hear.

Offer a closing prayer.

Dear God and Parent of us all, send us forth in grace and peace as we wait just a little longer for your matchless gift of love. Amen.

5. Love Is Born

BIBLE BACKGROUND

Praise God and give thanks that the long-awaited gift of God's love is here at last! A child has been born who Isaiah called the "Mighty God" and "Prince of Peace." This tiny baby lying in a manger is the One about whom the angel brought good news for all people. According to Luke, the first to hear were humble shepherds who rushed to see this child and bear witness to his parents as to what they had heard and seen. Titus prompts us to recall that we are living in the time between Jesus' first appearance as God-in-the flesh and the time when he will return again in glory. During this time, we are urged to live holy lives as those who have been saved by God's grace.

Isaiah 9:2-7

This week's text from Isaiah 9:2-7, along with Isaiah 11:1-10 (which we studied during the second week of Advent), are especially important to Christians because in these words we catch a vision of the messianic king. According to some scholars, these passages were incorporated into the coronation ritual, most likely for Hezekiah who ruled from 715—687 B.C. Other commentators dispute that idea and suggest that this hymn of thanksgiving was written after 732 B.C. to celebrate the birth of a new prince in David's line.

Differences of opinion existed among the Jewish people concerning the value of the monarchy. Those who highly regarded the Davidic monarchy and believed that a descendant of David would always occupy his throne also believed that when a king was crowned he was reborn as God's son (see 2 Samuel 7:14; Psalm 2:7-9; 89:19-29). Today's passage from Isaiah 9 fits perfectly with their idea of a righteous king. Centuries later, Christians would not only affirm that this is a vision of an ideal king but also claim that this king had come in the person of Jesus.

In 9:2-3, Isaiah pointed to the trouble the people had seen and the salvation that had come. In verses 4-7, the prophet explained why the people should celebrate and give thanks. God had saved the people from both military danger and political oppression (verses 4-5). The third reason for celebration is the birth of a male child who will reign with peace and justice.

The titles accorded to this child—"Wonderful Counselor, Mighty God, Eternal Father, Prince of Peace" (verse 6)—were not unique. When an Egyptian pharaoh was crowned, he was given similar titles. Pharaohs and other rulers of the Near East were regarded as divine.

The authority of this ruler will grow. So too will peace, justice, and right-eousness. This birth was a sign of hope, for it reaffirmed the promise made to King David that a descendant of his would always sit on the throne.*

Titus 2:11-14

Titus, along with 1 and 2 Timothy, are the three pastoral letters that tra-dition attributes to Paul. Titus and Timothy both assisted Paul in ministry. Titus helped to mediate the troubled relationship between Paul and the Corinthian church (see for example 2 Corinthians 7:6-7, 13-15).

Although not an explicitly Christmas text, today's epistle reading reflects on the meaning of God's grace "bringing salvation to all people" (verse 11). Jesus, referred to as "savior" in verse 13, made this salvation available to humanity. Believers acknowledge that salvation had already come when Jesus first appeared (verse 11). In addition, we look forward with hope to the appearance of Christ that is yet to come (verse 13). In the meantime, they are called to live "sensible, ethical, and godly lives" (verse 12) by rejecting the ungodliness of this world. God's grace "educates" us so that we may live as God intends (verse 12). As a result of Jesus' coming, people will be cleansed. Thus purified, believers are expected "to do good actions" (verse 14).

Titus reminds us that the coming of salvation in Jesus is not an event we simply celebrate and then forget as we go about business as usual. Instead, it has direct implications for the way we live each day. Those who belong to Christ—the church—have a responsibility to live in such a way that God's grace, which has enabled the coming of Christ, opens the way for all people to see the salvation that he brings. This is a message of hope. We cannot save ourselves, but Christ Jesus "gave himself for us in order to rescue us from every kind of lawless behavior" (verse 14). Thus, Titus helps us to tie together the Incarnation—God's gracious gift to us in coming in to earth as a helpless infant, "God with us"—and the Crucifixion and Resurrection that brought about our salvation through Jesus' self-giving on the cross. *

Luke 2:1-20

Luke anchored Jesus' nativity in the real world of first-century geogra-phy, economics, and politics. Caesar Augustus reigned sovereignly over the Roman Empire. To comply with his edict that one must return to one's home to be counted in a census for the purpose of taxation, Joseph and Mary left Nazareth and went to Bethlehem, the home of Joseph's ancestor King David. Scholars have been unable to find evidence of a worldwide census during the reign of Augustus, but Luke knew that Jesus had to be born in Bethlehem.

The text also invites comparisons between Augustus and Jesus. Augustus was widely hailed as a bringer of peace. The terms "Savior" and "Lord" applied to Jesus (verse 11, NRSV) had also been applied to Augustus. But the true Savior, Lord, and Prince of Peace was Jesus, not Augustus.

Although we hail Jesus as King of kings, his birthplace was humble, perhaps in a peasant home where the people slept upstairs and the animals slept below. His mother wrapped him snugly in bands of cloth, as was the custom of the day, and used an animal-feeding trough as his crib.

Jesus' first visitors were shepherds, whose job placed them at the bottom of the social ladder. Yet, as these ordinary men were going about their daily business of tending their flocks, an angel appeared and announced the "wonderful, joyous news for all people" (verse 10) that a savior had been born. Immediately, a heavenly choir praised God and declared peace on earth.

These shepherds then went to find the baby and speak with his parents. They found the holy, the sacred, not in the Temple in Jerusalem but in a humble place inhabited by peasants. The shepherds' response to what they had seen and heard was to share the good news and to praise God.

The wait is over. Let us join the heavenly host in giving praise and thanks that God's long-promised gift of love has arrived!*

SESSION PLAN

Open the Session

Celebrate the Messiah's coming with music.

Obtain a copy of George Frideric Handel's *Messiah* and an appropriate music player. Mention to participants that the words of this familiar oratorio come, in part, from Isaiah 9 and Luke 2, which are two of today's readings. Choose selections from the following: Air: Bass, Isaiah 9:2 (No. 11); Chorus, Isaiah 9:6 (No. 12); Recitative Soprano (No. 14a), Luke 2:8; Accompagnato Soprano (No. 14b), Luke 2:9; Recitative Soprano (No. 15), Luke 2:10-11; Reciative Soprano (No. 16), Luke 2:13; Chorus (No. 17), Luke 2:14. Invite participants to hum or sing along.

Ask: How does Handel's music help you to celebrate the birth of the Savior?

Offer an opening prayer.

Loving God, you loved the world so much that you gave us the gift of your beloved Son. We give you thanks, honor, and praise for this priceless baby who is "God with us." Empower us to live holy, sacramental, loving lives that befit those who call him Savior. Amen.

Engage the Scriptures

Praise God with the psalmist.

Distribute hymnals that include a Psalter or invite participants to turn to Psalm 96 in their Bibles. Read this psalm responsively.

Mention that this psalm of praise celebrated God's enthronement as the king who reigns as the savior, as the creator of the universe, and as the righteous judge.* Ask: How does this psalm embody the mood and meaning of Christmas Eve?

Discuss Isaiah 9:2-7

Call on a volunteer to read Isaiah 9:2-7. Read or review highlights of the Bible Background for this Scripture. Discuss the following questions:

1. How does the prophet Isaiah describe the people to whom the child of promise will be born?
2. How does Isaiah describe the child?
3. What changes will come about as a result of this child's coming?
4. Why do you think Christians have seen Jesus in these verses?

Explore the image of light.

Choose someone to read Isaiah 9:2-7. If possible, darken the room and provide a flashlight for the reader. Leave the room darkened and read the first two paragraphs of "Turn Toward the Light." Turn on the lights or open the curtains.

Invite participants to reflect silently on these questions:
1. Where in your life do you need light to shine? (pause)
2. How does the coming of the ideal, messianic king bring light into your darkness? (pause)
3. How does this light help you to feel God's love? (pause)

Conclude this activity by inviting volunteers to comment on discoveries they have made about the relationship between seeing the light and experiencing God's love?

Create graffiti sheets

Choose a volunteer to read Titus 2:11-14. Read or review highlights of the Bible Background for this Scripture.

Point out that God's grace not only brings salvation to all but also educates people so they may live in "self-controlled, upright, and godly" ways (verse 12, NRSV). Those who live this way "are eager to do good actions" (verse 14).

Post large sheets of paper around the learning area. Set out markers. Encourage participants to go to these sheets and create graffiti boards by writing words or phrases that for them indicate that someone is living a "sensible, ethical, and godly life." In addition, they may write specific actions that are indicative of such living. Call time. Suggest that everyone walk around to see what others have written and then return to their seats.

Ask:
1. What can we, as members of Christ's body, do to help one another live the kind of godly lives that we have described?
2. What can we do as a church to model this behavior so that more people will recognize that God's salvation is for all and thus be drawn into the body?

Consider the turnips

Read aloud the story about the man who dumped turnips on the church lawn in "Self-Control, Grace, and Love." Ask: Do you agree or disagree with the writer's response to the man's gift of turnips? Explain your response. How do you see God's grace and love at work in this story?

Roleplay the shepherds' response to good news.

Read aloud Luke 2:1-20 as participants close their eyes and try to imagine this scene.

Select two participants to act as roving reporters. The rest of the group will envision themselves as the shepherds. Encourage the reporters to pretend that they have hand-held microphones and move among the group to ask questions such as:

1. Can you describe for us what you saw and how you felt when you initially encountered the Lord's angel?
2. What thoughts crossed your mind when you realized that you were the first people to hear the announcement of the savior's birth?
3. We know you were in the fields tending your flock. That's your livelihood. So how did you and your colleagues decide to leave your flocks and go to Bethlehem? Weren't you worried about the sheep?
4. How did Mary and Joseph respond when you arrived unexpectedly?
5. How did Mary and Joseph react when you told them about the angelic visitation?
6. On the trip home, did you stop to tell anyone else? If so, how did they respond?
7. How would you say that your life has been changed because of this amazing news and your visit to the manger?

Sing a medley of carols.

Read or review highlights "Carol Your Way to Peace." Invite participants to comment on their own attachment to Christmas carols.

Distribute hymnals. Invite participants to call out the names and page numbers of carols that particularly relate to Luke's Nativity story. List the choices on a large sheet of paper. Here are some possibilities: "What Child Is This," "Angels We Have Heard on High," "Silent Night, Holy Night," "Away in a Manger," "Once in Royal David's City," "It Came Upon a Midnight Clear."

Encourage participants to look at the listed carols and select one or two verses from each that speak to them. Add verse numbers to the list. Sing as many carols as you have time for. If you do not have an accompanist, avoid carols that may be unfamiliar or difficult to sing.

Close the Session

Evaluate your Advent journey.

Encourage participants to thumb through GOD'S GIFT OF LOVE to review what they have read, the Scriptures they have studied, and activities and discussions over the last five weeks. Form teams and ask participants to discuss these questions, which you may wish to post on a large sheet of paper:
1. What has surprised you most about this year's study?
2. What questions remain unanswered for you?
3. How has this study enabled you to grow spiritually?
4. What will you share with others about your Advent journey?
Call participants together to thank them for being part of this study group and to wish them God's blessings in the year ahead. If other study opportunities are available, make them known or suggest that you will contact everyone when further information about a new study becomes available.

Offer a closing prayer.

O God, as we go forth to celebrate the birth of your Beloved Son, help us to remember that this gift of love came to set us free from the bonds of sin and death. Our journey that has brought us to Bethlehem's manger will continue to Golgotha's tree and end in victory at the garden of the empty tomb. Let your love continue to lead us each step of the way as we continue our own journey in faith. In Jesus' name we pray, Amen.

* Unless otherwise noted, all Bible Background information comes from *The New Interpreter's Bible*, *The New Interpreter's Study Bible*, or *The New Interpreter's Dictionary*.

Notes

1. From "Exegetical Perspective," by Bruce Birch from *Feasting on the Word*: page 53.
2. From "Fourth Conversation," *The Practice of The Presence of God*, by Brother Lawrence (Nicholas Herman), Grand Rapids, MI: Christian Classics Ethereal Library: page 13.
3. From "Second Conversation," *The Practice of The Presence of God*, by Brother Lawrence: page 7.

Preorder the new Lenten edition in the Series!

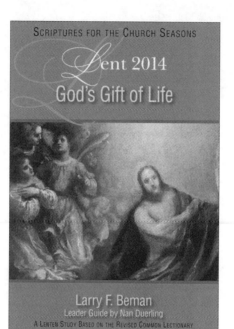

God's Gift of Life
A Lenten Study based on the
Revised Common Lectionary
Larry F. Beman, Nan S. Duerling

9781426768002

Scriptures for the Church Seasons series

⟨d⟩|Abingdon Press